THE CHISHOLM TRAIL IN AMERICAN HISTORY

William R. Sanford

Enslow Publishers, Inc.

40 Industrial Road   PO Box 38
Box 398   Aldershot
Berkeley Heights, NJ 07922   Hants GU12 6BP
USA   UK

http://www.enslow.com

Library of Congress Cataloging-in-Publication Data

Sanford, William, R. (William Reynolds), 1927–
    The Chisholm Trail in American history / William R. Sanford.
       p. cm. — (In American History)
    Includes bibliographical references and index.
    Summary: Presents the history of the trail which became the main route
for the Texas cattle trade after the Civil War.
    ISBN 0-7660-1345-6
    1. Chisholm Trail—History Juvenile literature. 2. Cattle drives—West
(U.S.) Juvenile literature. 3. Cowboys—West (U.S.)—History Juvenile
literature. 4. West (U.S.)—History Juvenile literature. [1. Chisholm
Trail. 2. Cattle drives. 3. Cowboys. 4. West (U.S.)—History.] I. Title.
II. Series.
F596.S224 2000
978—dc21   99-34973
                                         CIP

Printed in the United States of America

10 9 8 7 6 5 4 3 2

To Our Readers: We have done our best to make sure all Internet addresses in
this book were active and appropriate when we went to press. However, the
author and the publisher have no control over and assume no liability for the
material available on those Internet sites or on other Web sites they may link to.
Any comments or suggestions can be sent by e-mail to comments@enslow.com or
to the address on the back cover..

Illustration Credits: Enslow Publishers, Inc., p. 42; The Kansas State
Historical Society, Topeka, Kansas, pp. 8, 11, 20, 33, 47, 69, 73, 75, 81,
84, 88, 95; William R. Sanford, p. 6; Western History Collections,
University of Oklahoma Libraries, pp. 17, 26, 30, 32, 37, 39, 45, 56, 60,
62, 63, 78, 93, 97.

Cover Illustrations: © Corel Corporation; The Kansas State Historical
Society, Topeka, Kansas; Western History Collections, University of
Oklahoma Libraries.

★ CONTENTS ★

JOSEPH MCCOY HAS A VISION

The United States was at peace in 1867. Business was booming. The great Civil War had ended two years earlier. Joseph McCoy was a twenty-nine-year-old cattle dealer in Springfield, Illinois. He knew the cattle business from the ground up. He and his two older brothers, William and James, bought young cattle. Then they fed them until they were ready for market. Beginning in 1865, McCoy expanded his buying throughout central Illinois. He bought mules, cattle, sheep, and hogs in large numbers. The McCoy brothers sometimes shipped a thousand cattle a week. They bought them from $60 to $140 apiece. Their business quickly expanded outside Illinois. By 1867, the McCoys were shipping thousands of mature cattle to markets in the East.

McCoy Looks Ahead

Joseph McCoy had a vision. He knew he could buy Texas longhorns much cheaper than he was buying local cattle. He wanted to set up a location to which the longhorns could be driven. He talked with Charles

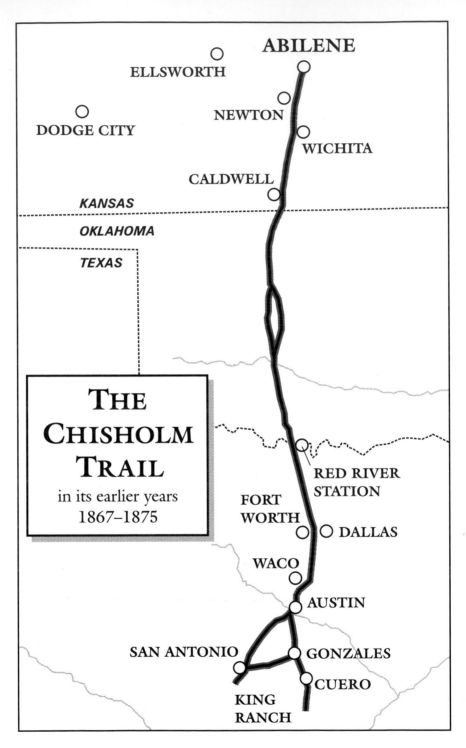

The Chisholm Trail

Gross, who had recently returned from Texas. Gross told him of millions of Texas cattle just waiting for someone to drive them to market. Early in 1867, McCoy bought some longhorns that had been driven north the year before. He saw that the hardy animals had survived the trail in good health.

McCoy thought about setting up his activities at Fort Smith, Arkansas, near the Oklahoma border on the Arkansas River. Texas cattle could be driven to eastern Oklahoma and Fort Smith (on the western border of Arkansas), using the Shawnee Trail. From there, cattle could be brought northeast to Cairo, Illinois, by steamboat. McCoy discovered that this was not a particularly good idea. The trip down the Arkansas River and up the Mississippi River would take many days. Housing and feeding large numbers of cattle on the small decks of the steamboats would be a major problem.

McCoy decided to investigate a location farther west. Kansas seemed an obvious choice. Kansas had been admitted to the Union in 1861. Only a few years earlier, Kansas had been a battleground between those who wanted the state to allow slavery and those who wanted the state to forbid it. The territory became known as Bleeding Kansas. Now there was peace. Like many other people who lived in Midwestern states, Kansans watched as railroads pushed westward. The railroads had received land grants for the many miles of track they laid. Now they needed to encourage new businesses and settlers to generate revenue for their new lines. The railroads were the key to McCoy's plan.

Joseph McCoy selected Abilene as his shipping point at the end of the Chisholm Trail. Abilene was a small town that had a dozen dirt-roofed log cabins and a few businesses.

Texas cattle could be bought cheaply at the end of the trail. If they could be shipped to market by railroad at a reasonable freight rate, there would be a nice profit for all concerned.

From St. Louis, McCoy took a Missouri Pacific train to Kansas City, Missouri. He talked with the owners of Marsh and Coffey, a firm that traded goods in the Indian Territory, as Oklahoma was then called. Marsh told McCoy that the Union Pacific Railroad had pushed as far west as Salina, Kansas.

McCoy Selects a Site

McCoy bought a round-trip ticket to Salina. On the way, the train was delayed for an hour in the prairie village of Abilene, Kansas. McCoy got off the train. He began asking locals about the suitability of that town as his shipping point. The citizens liked the idea at once. McCoy also investigated Kansas Falls, near Junction City, Kansas, where the Union Pacific Railroad offered to build him railroad tracks to the town. Local businessmen offered to give him five acres on which to build sheds and a stockyard. A railroad official orally promised to pay McCoy five dollars a head for all cattle shipped over the Union Pacific line that year.

McCoy did not make a quick decision. He needed to make a deal to get his cattle from the Union Pacific terminal in Kansas City, Missouri, to meat processing plants located farther east. McCoy did not fare well with the Missouri Pacific. He asked the railroad to give him a price quote on how much it would cost to ship large numbers of cattle from Kansas City to St. Louis. A railroad official questioned him closely. He learned that McCoy had not yet built pens or bought a herd. The official told McCoy, "You haven't any cattle to ship and never did have any; and I, sir, have no evidence that you ever will have any. . . . Therefore, you get out of this office, and let me not be troubled with any more of your style."[1]

McCoy had better luck with the Hannibal and St. Joseph Railroad, which gave him a good rate from Kansas City to Quincy, Illinois, and on to Chicago. This business decision had far-reaching consequences: Chicago, rather than St. Louis, became the site of the nation's largest stockyards and the home of the meat-packing industry.

McCoy decided on Abilene as his shipping point. He returned there in the middle of June 1867. The spring cattle drive season was almost over. There would be a second season in the fall. McCoy would have to act quickly if he wanted to ship many Texas cattle that year. Abilene consisted of a dozen dirt-roofed log cabins, and a few businesses, also built of logs. The largest, the Bratton Hotel, had six rooms. McCoy bought two hundred fifty acres on the northeastern edge of the village. From Hannibal, Missouri, he shipped in the lumber to build his stockyards. His carpenters finished the job in two months. He constructed a three-story hotel, the Drovers' Cottage, which offered a hundred rooms. Nearby, he built a large livery stable and a bank. McCoy was confident that if he built the facilities, the

Joseph McCoy built the Drover's Cottage Hotel to serve the cattlemen arriving in Abilene up the Chisholm Trail. It was three stories tall and offered a hundred rooms.

herds would come. McCoy hired surveyor Tim Hersey to lay out the route to his new town. With horses and oxen pulling plows, Hersey cut a wide trench eighty miles long from Wichita to Abilene.[2]

Problems for the New Town

The Abilene site gave McCoy a legal problem. Kansas was worried that the cattle belonging to Kansas farmers might be infected by diseases brought north by Texas cattle.[3] In February 1867, Kansas had drawn a north-south line across the state. Texas cattle could be driven to the railroad only west of that line. Abilene was sixty miles east of it. McCoy argued that the area around Abilene was thinly settled. There were few local farmers whose cattle might be infected by the Texas longhorns. McCoy got the support of Kansas governor Samuel Crawford. McCoy explained that almost all of the cattle trail to Abilene would lie west of Kansas settlements. The governor was convinced. He later remembered, "I wrote a plain, vigorous letter, commending Mr. McCoy's scheme and the location he had selected." Crawford added, "I approved of the undertaking in a semi-official manner."[4]

McCoy organized a campaign to bring cattle to Abilene quickly. He sent out handbills to towns throughout the southwest. In Texas newspapers, he placed advertisements that trumpeted the advantages of shipping from Abilene. McCoy also sent an Illinois stockman, W. W. Sugg, to follow up the ads. Sugg rode through the Southwest on horseback, repeating the message. McCoy learned that several large herds had left Texas and were trailing north. The trail bosses planned to hit the railroad at some unknown point. They had reason to be unsure. In 1866, Nelson Story, a lucky miner, cashed in his Montana gold for one thousand longhorns at Fort Worth, Texas. Then he drove them north across the Indian Territory. At the Kansas-Missouri border, his path was blocked by locals who were afraid that their stock would contract the Texas fever. Story had had to turn west and then north toward Montana.[5]

The First Herds Arrive

For the herds that had stopped in the Indian Territory, the wait was not all bad. The Texas spring had been a dry one. The cattle were thinner than usual. The delay allowed the cattle to gain weight by eating the ample grass of the open range. The local grass was plentiful, due to the high rainfall in the region that summer. McCoy obtained the services of several experienced plainsmen, who rode south into the Indian Territory to meet these herds and direct them to Abilene.

The riders found the herds south of the Arkansas River. The riders promised the Texans that they could drive their herds to Abilene without meeting resistance from local farmers and cattlemen. The riders' promises convinced the trail bosses. Though they were suspicious of McCoy's promises, they were tired of delay on the trail. They rounded up their grazing longhorns. Soon the lead steers had the herd plodding north toward Abilene.

Other Texas herds had gone to other Kansas towns. Colonel John Myers had brought a herd from Lockhart, Texas, to Junction City, twenty-four miles east of Abilene, where he awaited Illinois buyers.

Texas trail herds began arriving in Abilene in August. The promises the trail bosses had relied upon turned out to be valid. The herds had met with no opposition. There were cattle pens and buyers awaiting them. The first shipment of Texas longhorns left Abilene on September 1, 1867. They filled twenty railroad stock cars. The tracks headed east across Kansas to Junction City, through Fort Riley, and paralleled the Kansas River to Manhattan, Kansas. Farther east, the train and its historic cargo passed through St.

CENTRAL KANSAS WAS REVISITED FOR THE PURPOSE OF SELECTING A POINT AT WHICH THE FACILITIES FOR HOLDING, HANDLING AND SHIPPING CATTLE COULD BE MADE. FROM JUNCTION CITY, THE TRACK THE KANSAS PACIFIC RAILWAY WAS CLOSELY FOLLOWED, AND VARIOUS POINTS INSPECTED WITH REGARD TO THEIR ADAPTABILITY TO A CATTLE BUSINESS, UNTIL SOLOMAN CITY WAS REACHED, NEAR WHICH A FINE SITE FOR STOCK YARDS WAS FOUND; BUT AFTER ONE OR TWO CONFERENCES WITH SOME OF THE LEADING CITIZENS, IT BECAME EVIDENT THAT THEY REGARDED SUCH A THING AS A CATTLE TRADE WITH STUPID HORROR, AND FROM ALL THAT COULD BE LEARNED UPON THOROUGH INQUIRY, THE CITIZENS OF SALINA WERE MUCH IN THE SAME MOOD. THE PERSON MAKING SUCH PROPOSITIONS WAS APPARENTLY REGARDED AS A MONSTER THREATENING CALAMITY AND PESTILENCE. AFTER SPENDING A FEW DAYS INVESTIGATING, ABILENE, THEN AS NOW, THE COUNTY SEAT OF DICKINSON COUNTY, WAS SELECTED AS THE POINT OF LOCATION FOR THE COMING ENTERPRISE. ABILENE IN 1867 WAS A VERY SMALL, DEAD PLACE, CONSISTING OF ABOUT ONE DOZEN LOG HUTS, LOW, SMALL, RUDE AFFAIRS, FOUR-FIFTHS OF WHICH WERE COVERED WITH DIRT FOR ROOFING; INDEED, BUT ONE SHINGLE ROOF COULD BE SEEN IN THE WHOLE CITY. THE BUSINESS OF THE BURG WAS CONDUCTED IN TWO SMALL ROOMS, MERE LOG HUTS.[6]

In Joseph McCoy's autobiography, he told of how Abilene came to be the first cow town. In short, there were not many citizens in Abilene to oppose him.

Mary's and Topeka, Kansas, before reaching Kansas City, Missouri.

About thirty-five thousand cattle arrived in Abilene in 1867. The large number caused a sudden drop in beef prices in Abilene, Kansas City, and the eastern markets. Many owners decided not to sell their cattle at once. Only slightly more than half the cattle that reached Abilene that year were shipped east by train at once. The remainder spent the winter on the prairies west and north of the town.

The Texans who were able to sell their herds were delighted with the prices they received. When they returned to Texas, they spread the word quickly. Some there thought the news too good to be true. They wondered whether McCoy would turn out to be some kind of swindler. Mindful of their doubts, McCoy prepared for 1868 by again printing circulars describing the best route to follow to reach Abilene. He listed the facilities that awaited the herds there. McCoy also advertised in Midwestern newspapers to attract buyers. He promised that by mid May, buyers would find the best grazing cattle in the United States, weighing one thousand to thirteen hundred pounds apiece, at Abilene.

To get the cattle to Abilene, the trail bosses had to drive them up the Chisholm Trail.

★ DISCOVERING THE TRAIL'S NAMESAKE ★

There is one surprising fact about Jesse Chisholm: He never led a cattle drive up the trail that bears his name. The trader was born on Cherokee land, probably in Tennessee, about 1805 or 1806. His father was a Scottish white man, and his mother was half Cherokee. His family moved to Arkansas when Jesse was about ten. By the time he was twenty-six, he was hired by the United States government to lay out trails in the Indian Territory to the west. He helped survey a 147-mile trail through rough country from the Arkansas River south to Fort Towson, Oklahoma. The government used the route to send supplies to the Choctaw Indians.

In 1836, Chisholm married Eliza, daughter of trader James Edwards. Eliza died of smallpox in 1845. Her death left Jesse with a son, a daughter, and thirteen adopted children. His lifelong friend, Mrs. Shelton, moved into his home to care for the youngsters. Chisholm helped rescue a white boy captured by Comanches. The boy lived with the Chisholms and took the name George Chisholm.

Jesse Chisholm operated a trading post at the mouth of the Little River, near what is now Bilby, Oklahoma. He became the most successful trader on the South Plains. Apaches, Kiowa, and Comanches traveled long distances to trade in his store. Soon he was operating other trading posts near what are now Asher and Lexington, Oklahoma. He also owned a saltworks and operated a freight line. His travels took him to Texas, Mexico, and California.

Chisholm had great influence with the tribes of the Indian Territory. They regarded him as a friend they could trust. When the Civil War broke out in 1861, Chisholm advised the tribes to remain neutral. Unfortunately, not all

Jesse Chisholm had followed a trail north to trade with the Kiowa Indians. When Joseph McCoy used the same route for his cattle trail, it became known as the Chisholm Trail.

of them followed his advice. He himself maintained strict neutrality. Chisholm moved his family north, to a spot near present-day Wichita, Kansas. For years, he had used this route north to trade with the Kiowa. When the route was later followed by millions of cattle, it became known as the Chisholm Trail.

After the war ended in 1865, the government sought Chisholm out. Government officials wanted his help in negotiating treaties with the tribes that had gone to war.

Chisholm died in March 4, 1868, while he was on a trading expedition. According to some accounts, he died from food poisoning after eating bear meat cooked in a copper kettle. Others said Chisholm died of pneumonia.[7]

The Chisholm Trail linked two widely different regions of the United States. It originated in Texas, a former Confederate state. It ended in Kansas, which had sided with the Union. The trail was an example of the many links joining a reunited nation.

THE UNITED STATES IN 1867

The Nation

The United States in 1867 was binding up its wounds from the bloody Civil War (1861–65). The victorious Union army occupied the defeated Southern states. Vice President Andrew Johnson had become president of the United States after the assassination of President Abraham Lincoln.

Johnson, the former Democratic senator from Tennessee, soon found himself at odds with the Republican-controlled Congress. The lawmakers passed a civil rights act, giving citizenship to African-American men, and passed the Fourteenth Amendment to ensure its constitutionality. In 1867, overriding Johnson's veto, Congress passed the Reconstruction Act, which divided the South into five military districts.

Andrew Johnson was the president of the United States when the first herds came up the Chisholm Trail in 1867. He became president two years earlier, when Abraham Lincoln was assassinated.

The Reconstruction Act imposed martial law, and it placed requirements on Southern states seeking readmission to the Union. All states had to write new state constitutions that guaranteed universal manhood suffrage, the right to vote. The states also had to ratify the Fourteenth Amendment.[1]

Congress also passed the Tenure of Office Act in 1867. It limited the ability of the president to remove government officials from office. Johnson thought the law was unconstitutional. He defied the act by removing Secretary of War Edwin Stanton. In 1868, the Congress impeached Johnson. The president underwent trial in the Senate. The impeachment effort failed by one vote.

Nebraska was admitted to the Union in 1867, as the thirty-seventh state. Since 1860, Nebraska's population had quadrupled to one hundred sixty thousand. The population of the country was approaching 38 million. The center of the country's population had begun to move west. In 1867, it was located northeast of Cincinnati, Ohio. Immigrants were pouring into the country at a rate of over three hundred thousand a year. Nine out of ten came from northwestern Europe. Three out of four Americans lived in towns with fewer than twenty-five hundred people. No city had yet grown to a population of one million. Only two had passed five hundred thousand.[2]

In the mid-Pacific, the United States occupied the Midway Islands, west of Hawaii. In 1867, Secretary of State William H. Seward negotiated an agreement with Russia. The United States would buy the Russian possession of Alaska. Many Americans did not know what to make of the purchase. Opponents of the deal called it Seward's Folly and Seward's Icebox. They pictured Alaska as a wasteland of ice and snow. The purchase price was $7.2 million, about two cents an acre.

Life expectancy in 1867 was just over forty years. One baby in seven died in infancy, often from whooping cough or diphtheria. People of all ages died from cholera, smallpox, and typhoid fever.

Adult workers were organizing the first trade unions in this country. Their goal was an eight-hour day. The average industrial worker put in 10.8 hours per day at an average wage of about fifteen cents an hour.

Technology

By 1867, Americans were well into the Industrial Revolution. Mills driven by water power churned out consumer products in large quantities. The telegraph, invented decades earlier, linked the nation, coast to coast. After earlier failures, in 1866, a twenty-five-hundred-mile transatlantic cable successfully linked Europe to North America.

The country boasted over thirty thousand miles of railroads. Two thirds of the mileage was in the northern states. Railroad companies were beginning to replace their iron rails. The new steel rails were manufactured by the Bessemer process invented in England. Americans were traveling long distances in railroad sleeping cars invented by George Pullman. By November 1867, the Union Pacific tracks reached Cheyenne, Wyoming.[3] The

Union Pacific was building west from Nebraska toward Utah. There it would meet the Central Pacific, building east from California. The nation was only two years away from being spanned by a transcontinental railroad.

Petroleum products flooded the market after Edwin Drake's discovery of an oil field in Titusville, Pennsylvania. Soon, kerosene lamps lit every American home. The first pipeline was built in 1866. John D. Rockefeller became the country's first monopolist. He built refineries and bought up his competitors throughout the region.

Housewives were making widespread use of the mechanical sewing machine, which had been invented by Elias Howe and improved by Isaac Singer. The widespread success of condensed milk, patented by Gail Borden, encouraged a newly expanding food-processing industry. The Industrial Revolution reached even the rural areas. Horse-drawn agricultural machines, the harvester, reaper, and baler, were making large-scale farming practical.

Most local traffic was horse powered. In the cities, horse-drawn trolleys lined the streets. Business deliveries relied on horse-drawn vehicles. Rural dwellers traveled by carriage and wagon. When new states were carved into counties, the county seats were located within a day's travel by horse from any place within the county.

The South

Twenty thousand Union troops occupied the Southern states. The Reconstruction Act denied the right to vote to anyone who had held office under the Confederacy. This ban included even local officials. African Americans sat in every Southern state legislature. Some came under the influence of carpetbaggers and scalawags. Carpetbaggers were northerners who came south to seek their fortune. Scalawags were white Southerners who cooperated with the carpetbaggers. Some white Southerners joined the Ku Klux Klan. The secret organization adopted its constitution in May 1867. It chose former Confederate general Nathan B. Forrest as its Grand Wizard. The Klan used threats and violence to attempt to regain white supremacy. In 1870 and 1871, Congress passed the Ku Klux Klan Acts. The laws enforced the Fourteenth and Fifteenth Amendments, which had given citizenship and civil rights to former slaves.

In 1867, the Southern states were still suffering from the effects of the Civil War. An estimated 258,000 Confederate soldiers had lost their lives. Others returned from the war wounded or broken in health. They returned to a region whose economy had been based on cotton for half a century. After the war, cotton still played a major role. Cotton growers faced problems of war-ravaged railroads and mills, insects, and in 1867, a drought. With the end of slave labor, Southern planters faced a shortage of workers. Many landowners turned to sharecropping. The landowners provided former slaves with a place to live, seeds to plant, and tools. The workers continued to plant, weed, and pick the cotton, paying the landowners with most of the harvest.

Texas, the Confederacy's westernmost state, suffered under Reconstruction with the other Southern states. Thirty percent of its six hundred thousand people were former slaves. The Freedman's Bureau helped them find work. In 1867, Union Leagues helped enroll the new citizens in the Republican Party. Texas had elected former Confederate general James Throckmorton as governor. In 1867, a Union military commander, General Phil Sheridan, ordered him removed from office. Congress also denied membership to four former Confederates from Texas: three congressmen and a senator.

The West

In 1867, a vast unsettled area stretched between the western line of settlement in Kansas and Nebraska and the Rocky Mountains. Here, the Plains peoples were making a last desperate effort to maintain their way of life. The United States government was equally determined to end their freedom of movement, and to confine them to reservations.

The strength of the U.S. Army had dropped from over a million soldiers in 1865 to fifty-seven thousand two years later.[4] Those not on occupation duty in the South were scattered in forts across the frontier.

Along the Bozeman Trail that led from Wyoming to Montana, the army was losing a war to Red Cloud and the Oglala Sioux. The following year, the army abandoned Fort C. F. Smith and Fort Phil Kearney to the victorious Oglala.

On the treeless Western plains, farmers built their homes from sod.

Farther east, the railroads actively encouraged settlers to venture onto the plains. The government had rewarded the railroad builders by granting them millions of acres of land in return for expanding their track. The railroads needed farmers to ship goods along their lines. The railroads offered prospective settlers land at bargain rates.

The government too wanted the Western territory settled. The 1862 Homestead Act offered any citizen or person intending to be a citizen one hundred sixty acres of surveyed public land.[5] It asked for only five years of continued residence on the land, and payment of a registration fee of from twenty-six dollars to thirty-four dollars. Union army veterans with two year's service got their land after only living on it for two years. Those with money could gain title after six months' residence by paying $1.25 per acre.

Farmers throughout the West were unhappy with the railroads. They thought the freight rates they paid were too high. They claimed that the freight rates took away all their profits. In December 1867, the farmers set up the Patrons of Husbandry, whose members became known as Grangers. The organization attacked monopoly, railroads, and middlemen. It declared the need for colleges to teach agriculture.

The railroads hired professional hunters to kill buffalo to feed their building crews. Other hunters killed buffalo for their hides. The hides brought only one dollar to three dollars apiece. Within the next sixteen years, the buffalo herds were reduced from 13 million to a few hundred. The slaughter deprived the Plains peoples of their main food source. It aided the government in its drive to force American Indians onto reservations.

The East

The years immediately after the Civil War found the eastern states more prosperous than before. Many business owners had made their fortune making and selling supplies to the government. Cornelius Vanderbilt, for example, turned a small ferry business into a chain of steamships that dominated commerce on the East Coast. By 1867, his interest had shifted to railroads. He controlled the route between New York City and Albany, New York. Vanderbilt later extended his line west to Chicago.

American business was experimenting with a new form of organization—the corporation. It limited the owners' liability. It lived on after any individual's death. Through sales of stocks and bonds, it raised needed capital. By 1867, the New York Stock Exchange, founded in 1792, was providing the huge sums needed for the country's industrial expansion.

Though small towns continued to prosper in the East, the momentum shifted to the cities, where workers no longer toiled in their own fields and shops. They became wage earners. Factory owners looked on them as a commodity to be purchased as cheaply as possible. There began to be a greater spread between the wealth of the upper class and the poverty of lower class. The former lived in mansions, the latter in crowded tenements. A large middle class was made up of merchants and professionals.

Education for most children ended in elementary school. Of the more than 6 million students who attended elementary school, about one percent would go on to further education. The hungry factories of the East depended on an unending supply of cheap child labor. The hungry workers would be an excellent market for beef brought up the Chisholm Trail.

★ INVENTING RANCHING ★

In the years immediately following the Civil War, there were no cattle ranches in the United States. Cattle were raised on small farms, usually along with other cash crops. Even in the West, the government gave homesteaders only one hundred sixty acres, an area half a mile squared. The government required homesteaders to build a home, live there a number of years, and raise crops. Most homesteaders kept only a dairy cow or two to satisfy their own needs for milk, butter, and cheese. A nation hungry for beef found the supply of cattle to buy very limited. Most farmers who raised beef cattle had only a few to sell. They sold surplus beef only once a year.

In Texas, there was an unbelievably large supply of beef cattle. After Texas won its independence from Mexico in 1845, many Mexicans left their holdings north of the Rio Grande and moved south. For the next twenty years, the abandoned cattle roamed free. They became used to the harsh climate and multiplied. One estimate places the number of cattle in Texas in the late 1860s at 3 million. The cost of raising a steer to maturity in Texas was fifty cents a head, an amount that reflected the cost of branding it. There was little market for these cattle in Texas, even for their hides or tallow (used for making soap and candles).

The Texans quickly realized that if they were going to make money from cattle, they would have to be rounded up, branded, and transported on a large scale to the distant northern markets. Before they could do this, they would have to create a new agricultural organization. There was a model they could build on. This was the Mexican hacienda, a large self-contained rural landholding.

In Texas, ranchers raised vast herds of cattle. Their market lay far to the north—up the Chisholm Trail.

Each *hacienda* centered on a compound. It housed the owner's family, the workers, and the necessary workshops and storerooms. Many haciendas resembled high-walled square fortresses and provided their own defense. The workers, called *peones*, lived on the haciendas in near poverty, generation after generation.

Haciendas were not organized to raise large numbers of horses or cattle for export. To accomplish this, Americans invented the ranch. In the West, unfenced open range and plentiful grass allowed cattlemen to raise large herds. They managed the cattle from a central ranch headquarters. The annual roundup was followed by the trail drive to market. Texas longhorns would follow the Chisholm Trail to Kansas.

CATTLE ROUNDUP IN SOUTH TEXAS

The cattle that followed the Chisholm Trail to Abilene were gathered from many parts of Texas. South of Red River Station on the Indian Territory border, the Chisholm Trail spread out like branches from the trunk of a tree. The central segment of the trail network was most widely used. It began in the brush country of far South Texas, between the Nueces River and the Rio Grande. It passed near the cities of Austin, Waco, and Fort Worth. Another route led from the rocky Hill Country west of Austin. It was there that cowboys such as Sam Ealy Johnson, President Lyndon Johnson's grandfather, rounded up cattle for the drive north. To the east, feeder trails led from the grassy plains outside Houston.

In the 1860s, millions of cattle roamed South Texas. They were the descendents of cattle brought to the Americas by the Spanish in the 1500s. The first herd consisted of six Andalucian heifers and a bull, which were brought to Mexico in 1521. Twenty years later, the Spanish explorer Francisco Coronado headed

The Texas longhorns walked the lengthy Chisholm Trail and gained weight along the way. McCoy used the Chisholm Trail for the transport of longhorns to Kansas.

north from Mexico, seeking the gold of El Dorado. El Dorado was a mythical land said to be filled with riches. As he and his men crossed Texas and marched north, his men drove five hundred head of cattle. Many of the Spanish explorers who followed Coronado feared a food shortage in the unknown land. They also brought livestock with them. Some of the cattle escaped. Wandering in the wilderness, they became the nucleus of vast wild herds.

Slowly, the line of Spanish settlements in Mexico moved north. The pioneers brought their cattle with them to the frontier. For three centuries, the Spanish cattle mutated and evolved. On the haciendas, Mexican cowboys (called *vaqueros*) used terms that are still part of modern ranch talk today, although some have been changed in English. They include *lasso*, *corral*, *rancho*, *sombrero*, *quirt*, and *chaps*.

The Spanish settled in South Texas in the late 1700s. By then, there was a vast surplus of livestock. Wild herds of horses and cattle spread out into the rugged mountains to the west. Others grazed the grassy plains to the east. Many foraged in the sparse brush country north of the Rio Grande. By the time Texas won its independence in 1836, there were more

Cattle accompanied Francisco Vasquez de Coronado on his exploration of the Southwest in 1540. Many of the explorers who followed Coronado were afraid of a food shortage in the unknown land.

than six head of cattle for each Texan. There was no ready market for their meat. Texans slaughtered the cattle for their hide, tallow, hoofs, and horns. They left the carcasses to rot.[1]

Texas in the 1860s was thinly populated. Its population of over six hundred thousand was scattered over 266,807 square miles. Texas cities could not provide a market for all these cattle. Some Texans looked eastward toward Louisiana, where there were small markets in Shreveport and New Orleans. Ranchers had tried driving herds there before the Civil War. A few Texans trailed herds west to California to feed the gold-seeking forty-niners. One such drive took two years. The owners netted a twenty thousand dollar profit on eleven hundred longhorns. Those who tried to trail cattle to Missouri had less success. Troubles with farmers, American Indians, and thieves along the way discouraged many from attempting this route again.

Events that took place outside Texas changed the picture. In December 1865, the Chicago stockyards opened. At the 1,345-acre tract, nine railroads converged. Nearby were meat-packinghouses owned by Philip Armour, Michael Cudahy, and Franklin Swift. Two years later, Joseph McCoy arranged with the Kansas Pacific and Hannibal and St. Joseph railroads to transport cattle from his pens in Abilene to Chicago. For a long time, there had been a need for a market for Texas beef. The incentives to drive cattle north to Abilene had become irresistible.

A Question of Ownership

The laws of the Republic of Texas had made unbranded cattle public property. Legally, they were available for the taking. Each year there was a new crop of unmarked calves. Within months, these animals were weaned from their mothers. The yearlings roamed the brush country, prairies, and hill country. They became the property of the first person to find and brand them. The unbranded cattle were called mavericks. The name comes from Samuel Augustus Maverick, a San Antonio lawyer who owned a neglected ranch on Texas's Matagorda Bay. The buyer who purchased his cattle began branding all the unmarked stock he found anywhere nearby. People in the area started calling all unbranded cattle "mavericks." By 1867, most of Texas cattle had been branded by one person or another. Only in the brush country of South Texas were there many wild unbranded cattle remaining.

Some overzealous Texans began to intrude on their neighbor's ranges. They branded the calves they found there before the owners of the calves could brand the calves themselves. A November 1866 Texas law banned the practice, but the law was difficult to enforce. Mavericking continued until the late 1880s, when Texas law equated it with stealing.

Brands date back thousands of years to ancient Egypt. More recently, in the 1500s, the Spanish explorer Hernán Cortés burned his brand, a cross, on the flanks of the animals he brought to Mexico. Many owners named their ranches after their brands.

Even the greenest cowboy quickly learned to read the three elements of the branding alphabet. A brand is read from left to right, from top to bottom, or from outside to inside. For instance, a star inside a circle becomes the Circle Star, not the Star Circle. Brands consisted of letters, numbers, and a variety of combinations of both. Others used geometric symbols, or pictorial symbols.

Brands had their own terminology. An upside-down letter was termed *crazy*. One at right angles was *lazy*. If the letter was tilted, it was *tumbling*. A quarter circle under a brand made it *rocking*. The same symbol on the top became *swinging*. A horizontal line was a *bar*. A diagonal line was a *slash*.

Applying the Brand

The traditional spot on a cow's hide for branding was the left rear hip. Some owners branded their cows on the ribs, the right hip, or both hips.

To brand cattle, a group of about six cowboys would herd a couple hundred head of cattle and their calves toward an open space where a narrow band of white smoke rose from a branding fire. Its coals glowed bright red. It heated the branding end of the irons placed upon it. The cowboys circled the herd about fifty yards away. Two skilled cowboys mounted their horses with their *reatas* (roping lassos). Working as a team, they cut a calf from the herd, then snared the animal with a loop. Smoothly they dragged the animal toward the fire. A third cowboy on foot grabbed the rope. He might lift the calf around the middle and throw it to the ground. He might choose to grab and pull sidewise on its tail, throwing the calf off balance and toppling it.

The cowboy held the calf to the ground. A fourth cowboy picked up a hot iron. He quickly placed the brand against the calf's flank. There was the scent of burning hair and flesh. The calf bawled loudly in protest. Another cowboy placed his boot on the calf's head. He used his sharp knife to cut a distinctive notch in the calf's ear. If the calf was male, this cowboy finished the job by snipping off its testicles. He applied creosote, used as an antiseptic, to the wound to keep the flies away. When the calf was released, it scrambled to rejoin its mother. By then, another roped calf was

Roping and branding cattle before they headed north on the Chisholm Trail required a team effort. Branding was used to mark cattle. Unbranded cattle were public property.

being dragged to the fire, where the process was repeated.

The Roundup

Cattle grazed in small groups or by themselves. The first job for a prospective traildriver was to round the cattle up into large herds. In South Texas, the cattle hid out in the thick brush of thorny chapparal and mesquite during the day. They ventured out on the prairies only at night. The cowboys mounted up before daylight to seek the strays. They rode to the edge of a chosen thicket, a dense growth of trees or shrubs. At first light, they would approach the cattle still out on the prairie.

An old steer would spot the riders as soon as they approached. The whole bunch would stampede directly at the riders positioned between them and their shelter. Every man selected an animal to rope and tie down. If time permitted, the riders would go to another thicket and repeat the process.

Other cowboys drove up the main herd of cattle gathered earlier. When the main herd surrounded the animals that had been tied down, they were released. Generally, they were content to stay with the herd. If an animal made a break for the brush, it was roped again. Then its eyelids were sewed shut until it became docile.[2]

After a rancher collected his herd, he usually sold it to a cattle dealer, a middleman who combined the cattle from several ranches to build their numbers to a size

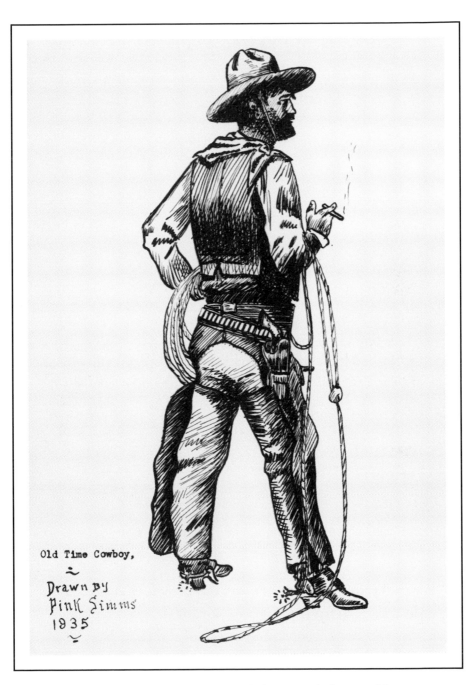

Old Time Cowboy,
Drawn by
Pink Simms
1935

Cowboys developed distinctive clothing: Wide-brimmed hats, leather vest and chaps, high-heeled boots, and spurs.

SOURCE DOCUMENT

I WAS SIXTEEN YEARS OLD. WE WERE SNARING *LADINOS*[3] OUT OF THE ARTILLERY THICKET AND HAD GONE OUT BEFORE DAYLIGHT TO WAYLAY THEM ON AN OPENING. AFTER DAWN, WE SIGHTED A LITTLE BUNCH MOVING BACK TOWARDS THE BRUSH. I TOOK AFTER WHAT PROVED TO BE A BULL FIVE OR SIX YEARS OLD. A JUMP OR TWO BEFORE MY HORSE STARTED GOING DOWN A HILL, I THREW THE LOOP. THE HORSE SQUATTED, THE ROPE TIGHTENED, AND MY CINCH BROKE.

WHEN THE SADDLE LEFT, I WAS STILL STRADDLING IT AND I KEPT RIGHT ON STRADDLING IT. IT HIT THE GROUND STRAIGHT, AND I RODE THAT SADDLE FOR WHAT SEEMED TO ME TO BE A QUARTER OF A MILE, THOUGH IT TURNED OUT TO BE ONLY ABOUT A HUNDRED YARDS. IT WAS MOVING TOO. SOON THE BULL, THE SADDLE, AND I GOT ALL TANGLED UP IN THE BRUSH. I GOT OFF. THE SADDLEHORN AND THE ROPE HELD. THE BULL WAS A FIGHTER. WE SEWED HIS EYES UP WITH FOUR STITCHES OF BUCKSKIN TO EACH PAIR OF LIDS AND TOOK HIM OUT WITH A BUNCH OF GENTLE CATTLE.

NO, I WASN'T HURT—JUST SCRATCHED UP A LITTLE BIT AND BRUISED IN A FEW PLACES.[4]

Here is a description of a roundup as given by cowboy Rocky Regan.

suitable for being driven on the trail to Kansas. The dealers recruited the cowboys for the drive and selected the trail boss. The dealers took all the financial risks, and all the profits belonged to them as well.

A large ranch owner might choose to take charge of the trail drive himself. From his South Texas ranch,

Richard King sent more than one hundred thousand steers up the trail in herds of from one thousand to four thousand. King made his trail bosses partners in the drive. Before heading north, they signed a note (a promise to pay debt) for the herd at its Texas value, in addition to the value of the horses and equipment.

On an 1875 trail drive, trail boss John Fitch signed for 4,737 cattle and 137 horses. Four months later, Fitch sold the cattle for eighteen dollars a head. His share of the profits was $5,366. At the time, this represented several years' earnings for most men. Raising the cattle had cost Richard King less than two dollars a head. He collected $61,886, of which more than fifty thousand dollars was profit.[5]

King himself never accompanied his herds as they followed the Chisholm Trail to Kansas. Those who did might have told him that he had missed one of life's great adventures.

★ "GIMME MY BOOTS AND SADDLE!" ★

Although his employer owned his horse, a cowboy owned his boots and saddle. They were often his most prized possessions. The boots were usually custom made, sometimes costing more than fifty dollars a pair—two months' salary. The boots evolved from the flat-heeled round-toed boots brought home from the Civil War. They became specialized and functional in design. The *tops* were generally about seventeen inches long. They protected the legs from saddle burn and thorny underbrush.

The foot section of the boots was made skintight. Cowboys wanted to be sure no one confused them with big-footed farmers. The *pointed toes* were more than stylish—they allowed the cowboy to insert the boot quickly and easily into a swinging stirrup.

The *boot heels* were narrow, high, and sloped to hold the stirrup firmly. They were also a safety device. If there was trouble, the higher heels prevented the rider's foot from slipping through the stirrup and the rider from being dragged by a runaway horse.

A traditional part of every cowboy's image was his highly practical metal *spurs*. The semicircular band of the spur fit over the back of the boot. A jingling chain passed under the heel and kept the spur from rising up. A spur strap, fitted across the instep, kept the spur firmly in place. The spurs usually had smoothed-off *rowels* to avoid scarring the cowboy's horse.

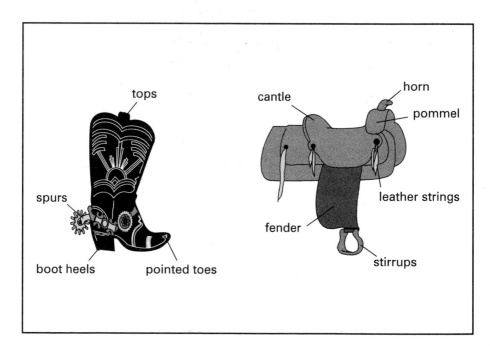

By the mid 1880s, boots took on more frills—fancier leathers, elaborate stitching, and floppy straps for pulling them on.

Cowboys lived in their saddles all day, and often part of the night. A well-made saddle cost roughly a month's wages. The cowboy's working saddle differed greatly from the English saddle common in the East. Built on a wooden frame, the cowboy's saddle had a high pommel in front and a tilted cantle in back, which helped to keep the rider in the saddle.

Broad leather fenders protected the rider's legs from the sweat of his mount. The large stirrups were made of bent wood, which was stronger than a solid piece. The leather-covered metal horn was the anchor pin around which the rider twisted his lasso when he was roping. Leather strings allowed the rider to fasten his rolled-up slicker or other gear behind him.

At night, the saddle became the cowboy's pillow. The saddle was so vital to the cowboy's work, that the saying "He's sold his saddle" meant that the man was a cowboy no longer.

4

LIFE ON THE TRAIL

A typical day for a trail crew on the Chisholm Trail might find them hundreds of miles and several weeks from home. Back in Texas, many cowboys had jumped at the chance to join a drive up the Chisholm Trail. They hoped it would be the adventure of their lives. They learned their lesson within the first days out. Driving cattle from Texas to Abilene was a hard way to make a hundred dollars. Most made the round-trip only once. Most were young, many in their teens. Many were former Confederate soldiers. Of the estimated thirty-five thousand cowboys who worked the ranches and rode the trails, over five thousand were African American. They participated in almost all the drives north. African Americans filled every job except that of trail boss. On a few cattle drives, the entire crews were black except for the white trail boss. Many of the African Americans had been slaves on Texas ranches, where they had learned their roping and riding skills. An equal number of Mexicans worked as cowboys.[1] For all of the cowboys, a typical day on the trail was much the same.

Early Morning

The eastern glow of first light on the prairie usually revealed a chuck wagon surrounded by sleeping men. The silence would be broken by one man, the cook, who rose before dawn to work with his pots and pans. His wake-up call contained a warning: If the cowhands did not stir themselves as fast as he would like, he would toss their breakfast into the creek. For some of the cowboys, the night's sleep had been brief. They had completed their night guard shift less than three hours earlier.

Even after dawn, two night guards circled the bedded-down cattle. Walking their horses slowly, the guards rode in opposite directions. In camp, the wakened cowboys pulled on wool shirts, fabric pants, and

Cowboys ate their meals sitting on the ground near the chuck wagon. The cook was always the first to wake up in the morning.

boots. They got water to wet their faces from the spigot of the water barrel on the chuck wagon. There was only one towel for them to share. The cowboys took one-pint tin cups from the lid of the chuck box at the back of the wagon. From the dropped lid of the chuck box, they helped themselves to bacon and corn bread. They ate seated on the ground nearby, sitting with folded legs, tailor style. By 5:15 A.M., the cowboys had finished their meal and drunk their black coffee. It was time to mount.

Two cowboys would hold ropes tied to the chuck wagon's wheels to form a corral. It was the wrangler's job to drive in the cowboys mounts for the day. The horses were gentle. They allowed the cowboys to approach with a halter. Each cowboy bridled and saddled a horse. Before mounting, the cowboys tossed their bedrolls into the chuck wagon. Two of them rode to relieve the night guards. Once off duty, the guards would dash into camp. They stayed only long enough to gobble their breakfast before returning to their saddles. The cook slammed the chuck box shut. It was time for him to drive off toward the noonday meeting place.

Moving Out

Nearby lay the Chisholm Trail. It had taken only a few years of use for the hooves of a million head of cattle to wear the trail below the level of the plains. In places, the trail stretched from two hundred to four hundred yards wide. From horseback, the cowboys would move the cattle onto the well-trodden trail. They did not want the cattle to walk through the dew-laden grass, because the moisture would soften their hooves. The cattle assumed a ragged line of march. Gradually the line would thin out to four or five abreast. It lengthened to almost two miles. Riders on both sides and at the rear of the column kept the line firm. They chased back any strays and urged the cattle forward. At the front, specially selected lead animals plodded patiently. They showed the way for the others to follow. Only the lead

On the trail, the herd of Longhorns could stretch out over a mile. The trail boss led the herd. He was in charge of the drive. For one hundred dollars a month, he was expected to ensure the safety of the herd at all times.

cattle would keep the cowboys company on their return ride home.

Usually there were enough riders to handle the cattle comfortably. Cattlemen who owned the herds wanted to be sure the cattle were well cared for. Some owners hired one cowboy for every two hundred fifty head of cattle. Others thought that one per four hundred was enough.

The trail boss rode up ahead. He was completely in charge of the drive. For his one hundred dollars a month, he was expected to ensure the safety of the herd at all times. Most likely, he was the only member of the drive who could read and write with ease. His job included keeping accurate records of the trip. His duties were many.

> He must see that there are enough provisions, as short grub does more toward dissatisfying the cowboy than anything else. He must assign each man to his proper duty. He must be the first one up in the morning. He must ride ahead to see that there is water at the proper distance. He must know where to stop for noon. He must count the cattle at intervals to see that none have been lost. He must settle all difficulties with his men.[2]

In Kansas, the trail boss would negotiate for a sale price.

The men took turns riding in the different positions. Behind the trail boss, near the head of the column, rode pairs of point riders. Swing and flank riders rode on either side, farther back. The riders bringing up the rear had the least desirable spot. They wore bandannas over their faces to cope with the dust.

These cowboys constantly had to harass calves and weaker animals to make them keep up, cracking the buckskin popper on the end of their rope. One cowboy remembered that the best place to learn new cusswords was at the tail of the herd. The wrangler rode off to one side of the herd. Often he was the youngest member of the group. For his twenty-five dollars a month, he served in camp as the cleanup and errand boy for the cook. On the trail, he escorted the drive's eighty horses, purchased back in Texas for fifteen dollars apiece.

The cattle moved slowly, scarcely more than a mile or two per hour. It did not take long for the cattle to assume their accustomed place in the line. Each day found the same cattle near the front, middle, or back of the herd. The weather was usually hot, the sky cloudless. The riders plodded their weary way until they saw the chuck wagon, camped near a spring. It was 11:00 A.M., time for "nooning," a period for eating and resting. The herd stopped, broke out of its long file, and began to graze. The wrangler released his string of horses to do likewise.

The grass on which the cattle fed was called buffalo grass, a soft velvety kind that seldom grew over three or four inches tall. The blue-green grass attained its full growth in spring during the rainy season. It dried up in the summer, but retained its nutrition.

Midday Break

Most of the cowboys rode to the chuck wagon. Dismounting, they dropped their reins in front of their horses. Their mounts stood patiently in place. The wrangler began his search for firewood for cooking the noon meal. He hoped to find dry limbs close to camp. Wrapping his rope around the saddle horn, he would drag the small limbs to the campfire. The cowboys sat near the campfire. There often was no shade except that furnished by the wide bands of their sombreros.

The meal offered no surprises. The menu of beef, beans, and biscuits seldom varied. The coffee came in packages that included a piece of hard candy. When the cook called out, "Who wants to grind the coffee today?" there would be a rush of volunteers. The grinder got the piece of candy.

After their meal, the wrangler drove up fresh mounts. The cowboys shifted their saddles and bridles to their new mounts. Those cattle that had finished grazing and were lying down were urged to their feet. The trail boss hurried them along. He had learned that another herd was coming up from behind his. He did not want to risk mixing the two herds; nor did he want the other herd to beat him to the grazing point he had selected for that night. He urged the cowboys to get their herd in motion quickly. Within minutes, the cattle were plodding north.

Afternoon

As the afternoon wore on, not a breath of air was stirring. Thousands of hooves raised a dense plume of dust that drifted slowly upward in a solid cloud. Riders at the back of the herd covered the lower part of their faces with their bandannas. The dust caked on every part of them and their horse that was exposed. Perspiration ran down the flanks of the horses. A ring of sweat lather surrounded their headbands and saddles. By the time they stopped for the night, both cowboys and horses were tired. They had traveled fourteen miles that day.

Their campsite was by a small stream. The cattle gathered there to drink. Then they spread out, searching for grass to graze on. The cowhands who were not on guard duty headed upstream. Stripping to their underwear, they bathed, then washed their dusty clothes. Changing into their spare outfit, they hung the washing on bushes to dry. Then they drifted back to camp.

Evening

The cook had arrived an hour earlier. His menu repeated what he served for the midday meal and supper the day before and the day before that. The cook had no choice. No one criticized the food. The evening meal was soon over. The cook washed the plates and refilled the water barrels. He checked the scab of a deep cut on one cowboy's arm, to make sure there was no sign of infection. The cowboys rolled and packed their washed clothing. The fire of dry limbs was allowed to die down. Everyone was weary. The evening pastimes of storytelling, card playing, equipment mending, and singing were dispensed with. As soon as it was dark, the first pair of night guards went on duty. The

WE WERE ALMOST WORN OUT STANDING NIGHT GUARD HALF OF EVERY NIGHT FOR THE PAST MONTH AND THEN STARTING IN WITH A FRESH OUTFIT MADE IT APPEAR TOUGH TO US.

THAT NIGHT IT BEGAN TO STORM TERRIBLY. THE HERD BEGAN TO DRIFT EARLY AND BY MIDNIGHT, WE WERE FIVE OR SIX MILES FROM CAMP. THE STEERS SHOWED A DISPOSITION TO STAMPEDE BUT WE HANDLED THEM EASY AND SANG MELODIOUS SONGS, WHICH KEPT THEM QUIETED. BUT ABOUT ONE O'CLOCK THEY STAMPEDED IN GRAND SHAPE. ONE OF THE "SHORT HORNS" [INEXPERIENCED COWBOYS], A LONG LEGGED FELLOW BY THE NAME OF SAINT CLAIR GOT LOST FROM THE HERD AND FINALLY WHEN HE HEARD THE SINGING CAME DASHING THROUGH THE HERD AT FULL SPEED YELLING "LET 'EM SLIDE [STAMPEDE], WE'LL STAY WITH 'EM!" AT EVERY JUMP.

THEY DID SLIDE SURE ENOUGH, BUT HE FAILED TO "STAY WITH 'EM." FOR TOWARDS MORNING ONE OF THE BOYS CAME ACROSS HIM LYING IN THE GRASS SOUND ASLEEP. WHEN HE CAME DASHING THROUGH THE HERD A STAMPEDE FOLLOWED. THE HERD SPLIT UP INTO A DOZEN DIFFERENT BUNCHES—EACH BUNCH GOING IN A DIFFERENT DIRECTION. I FOUND MYSELF ALL ALONE WITH ABOUT THREE HUNDRED OF THE FRIGHTENED STEERS. OF COURSE, ALL I COULD DO WAS TO KEEP IN FRONT OR IN THE LEAD AND TRY TO CHECK THEM UP. I FINALLY ABOUT THREE O'CLOCK GOT THEM TOPPED AND AFTER SINGING A FEW LULLABY SONGS THEY ALL LAY DOWN AND WENT TO SNORING.[3]

In his 1885 book, A Texas Cowboy, *trail hand Charles A. Siringo remembered the end of a day's work on the Chisholm Trail.*

remaining cowboys spread their blankets. They used their saddles as pillows. Soon, all were fast asleep.

Before turning in, the trail boss, ever alert, noticed indications of a storm. He walked out of camp and surveyed the sky to the west, where he saw a dark rolling cloud in the night sky. He instructed the night watch to wake him at the first sign of lightning. That night he was lucky. After the trail boss returned to his bedroll, the cloud passed over quietly. The cowboys were not required to deal with a stampeding herd.

★ "Come 'n Get It!": The Chuck ★ Wagon and the Cook

The chuck wagon was the center point of every night's camp. It carried the cowboys' bedrolls and spare clothing, as well as cooking gear and several months' supplies of groceries. The four-wheeled wagon was usually pulled by four horses or mules. Cooks preferred wagons with wide tires for better traction in rough country. Supplies protected by canvas stretched over hoops filled the center of the wagon. Under the wagon, a hammock carried dry wood for starting fires. It carried a barrel of fresh water, and sideboards for bedrolls. At the back was a multi-drawer chuck box. From it, a hinged shelf swung down to form the cook's working area.

Second only to the trail boss, the cook was vital to the drive's success. The cook did more than prepare meals. He ordered supplies, loaded the wagon, and drove it across all types of terrain. He served as the camp doctor, setting broken bones, spooning out patent medicines for stomach problems, and dosing cuts with homespun cures (such as kerosene). He performed repairs on tattered clothing, settled arguments and bets, and stored valuables. As the crew neared the end of the drive, or whenever the cowhands received an invitation to a nearby ranch, the cook served as a barber, providing shaves and haircuts.

The cook was up early each morning, preparing the first of three hot meals he served to the score (twenty) or more cowboys every day. He rolled out of his blanket roll well before daylight, built a campfire, and began brewing coffee. The standard dishes prepared in the cook's cast iron Dutch ovens were baking-powder biscuits, beans, and bacon. The cook had to possess the knack of making do with the staples available, and making it tasty. A bad cook could cause cowboys to drift away from the outfit that employed him. After breakfast, the cook rode ahead of the herd to the midday resting spot, where he would serve lunch. In the afternoon, he was again on the move to that night's campground. At night, the cook would often stay up until everyone except the night guard was bedded down. His last chore of the day was to point the tongue of the chuck wagon toward the North Star. This gave the trail boss a compass heading the next morning.

Trail driving built healthy appetites. There was little delay when the cook bawled out, "Come 'n' get it before I throw it out!"

HAZARDS OF THE TRAIL

No cowboy ever mistook the trail drive for a cross-country picnic. Danger, illness, and death were constant companions. A quietly grazing herd could stampede without a second's notice. A small stream could turn into a raging torrent without warning. A flick of a longhorn's head could inflict a serious wound. Nature seemed to furnish an oversupply of creatures eager to bite the trail crew. A wet season left pools of water on the hard-packed trail. Mosquitoes multiplied. Despite the warmth of the evenings, trail hands clustered nightly around the campfire. They counted on its smoke, and that of their pipes, to keep the winged pests at bay. In the morning, cowhands were careful to shake their boots to check for scorpions lurking there.

Snakes, Falls, and Illnesses

No boot reached high enough to protect against the lunge of a giant rattlesnake. At night, rattlers sometimes sought out the warmth of a cowboy's bedroll. The sleeper might awake to find the rattler already coiled. It would sound its warning rattle, ready to

A herd standing quietly could break into a stampede without any warning. A stampede occurred when each animal in the herd ran because it believed another animal had seen a life-threatening danger.

strike at any sudden movement. Snakes hidden in the grass were ever-present threats to the unprotected legs of the horses.

A night guard's horse could also unwittingly step into a prairie dog hole, stumble, and pitch the half-asleep rider to the ground. In that situation, a rider who was not trampled thought himself lucky. More common was the fracture of a collarbone or a couple of ribs.

The hardships of the trail wore down the resistance of the healthiest of young men. Doctors were seldom available to set broken bones or prescribe medication. In an area where streams were scarce, there was a need to use the same stream for drinking water, bathwater, and toilet. The trail drivers had to ignore the fact that countless steers were doing the same. Inevitably, this led to cholera. Though limited only to humans, the highly infectious disease was usually fatal. In the United States, 1867, 1873, and 1884 were epidemic years. In 1869, cholera was widespread among the American Indians of southern Kansas. In time, the disease spread to the cowboys on the Chisholm Trail.

Storms Could Bring Death

Nature seemed to save its worst for the trail herds. Thunder and lightning caused more stampedes than did anything else. Lightning killed both cattle and cowboys. During a fierce downpour, it might seem like a good idea to seek any available shelter. In 1870, two trail hands rode under a tree during a thunderstorm. A single lightning bolt killed them both.[1] In a storm, balls of electricity, known as Saint Elmo's fire, sometimes would leap snakelike across the steers' horns.

Despite the assurance that spring begins in late March, trail herds that headed north in April sometimes got a surprise. In April 1874, two outfits camped on Hell Raising Creek in the Indian Territory. They lost their entire string of horses during one night of wind-driven snow and sleet.[2]

Around campfires, cowhands exchanged tales of the size of the hailstones that pelted them from time to time. The hailstones, often the size of golf balls, killed many cattle. Wise cowboys stripped the saddles from their mounts and took shelter under them. They listened helplessly as the hailstones struck the cattle with dull thuds. It was as if rocks had been thrown against them with great force. Hailstones stunned and gashed the heads of riders caught in the open. A blow on a cowboy's hand left it numb and almost useless.

Windstorms sometimes overturned chuck wagons and blew away tents. Downpours caused flash floods. After a rain, streams sometimes rose several feet within a few minutes. Dry washes became life-threatening torrents. Prairie fires were started by lightning, careless cooks, or American Indians. The fires frequently caused delays and detours, but seldom caused loss of life.

The Dreaded Stampedes

The most dangerous phenomenon on the Chisholm Trail was the cattle stampede. This panic-stricken rush of animals occurred when each animal in the herd ran because it believed some other animal had seen a life-threatening danger. The chance of stampedes increased as the cattle were called on to face a new experience. It could be as simple as a Texas housewife shaking her apron at a cow eating her flower border as the herd passed her ranch house. The most dangerous times were when it was extremely dark, or when a storm was about to break. A clanging pan, a sudden roll of thunder, or a skulking coyote could set the herd in motion. At times like this, riders tried to distract the attention of the herd by circling them, and singing for hours on end. Despite their efforts, in one jump, the cattle would be on their feet and running. The cowboys could only loosen their reins, grab their saddle horns, and trust in their surefooted mounts.

Running cattle always turned slowly to the right. Even in a stampede, they followed their leaders. The night ponies knew the ways of longhorns. At a full run, the ponies would edge along the left side of the herd. Some nights the riders were fortunate. The herd would not spread out too wide. When the riders reached the lead animals, they pressed them into turning sharply to the right. The herd would begin to pinwheel, then walk slowly in a tight group. When the herd stopped running, the cowboys could spread them out by separating small groups from the herd. Only then would they try to get the cattle to bed down for the night.

Perilous River Crossings

It was not stampedes that killed the most cattle. It was the many river crossings a herd had to make along the Chisholm Trail. The larger streams included the Colorado, Brazos, and Red Rivers in Texas, the Canadian and North Canadian and Cimarron Rivers in Indian Territory, and the Arkansas River in Kansas. In addition, there were dozens of smaller creeks and streams along the way. Crossing them was a test of skill. If the river was low, the cattle were in danger of

Crossing rivers was hazardous for cowboys and cattle on the Chisholm Trail. If the river was low, the cattle were in danger of being caught in quicksand. If it was high, the cattle had to swim across.

being caught in quicksand. If the water was high, the cattle were made to swim across.

It was the trail boss's responsibility to select the point for crossing streams. The lead cattle were directed to this point. They usually approached the stream slowly, plunged in, and headed straight for the opposite bank. The herd unhesitatingly followed its leaders. Trail bosses learned not to begin river crossings late in the day when the sun was low and facing them. Then the cattle sometimes started milling halfway across the stream, and many drowned. Cowboys broke up a milling herd by riding into its middle, yelling, and slapping the animals. Sometimes cowboys were caught midstream in a herd of milling cattle, knocked from their horses, and drowned.

The Red River was extremely dangerous to cross. It could rise rapidly, catching herds while they crossed. The Cimarron had a bottom of quicksand that snared any steer that stopped to drink. Pulling cattle from quicksand was slow, hard work. On the banks of other streams, there were deposits of gypsum that poisoned the cattle. If the streams were too high or the current too swift to allow the cattle to swim safely, the herds

SOURCE DOCUMENT

THE CANADIAN, THE WORST RIVER ON THE ENTIRE DRIVE, HAVING BEEN CROSSED WITHOUT ANY DIFFICULTY, ALL HANDS AND THE BOSS WERE HAPPY AND LIFE LOOKED BRIGHT ON "THE LONE COW TRAIL." TRUE, EVERY MAN IN THE OUTFIT, EXCEPT THE COOK, WAS SOAKING WET, BUT THEY WOULD SOON DRY, AND THAT MATTERED NOT. IN FACT, THE SITUATION WAS TAKEN INTO ACCOUNT AS SOON AS EVERYTHING WAS ON THE NORTH BANK, AND THE RIDERS BRINGING OVER THE WAGON, NOT HAVING BEEN ABLE TO BOUNCE THE COOK OUT OF THE SPRING SEAT AND GET HIM WET, GATHERED HIM UP BODILY AND CARRIED HIM BACK AND THREW HIM HEADLONG INTO THE RIVER. THEY DECLARED THAT NO "STUCK UP" COOK COULD MARCH AROUND ALL SWELLED UP WITH DRY CLOTHES ON HIS BACK WHEN ALL THE REST OF THE OUTFIT, INCLUDING "THE MADE-TO-ORDER COW-PUNCHERS," WERE SOAKING WET.[3]

A trail crew engages in horseplay after a dangerous river crossing.

If the river was shallow enough, the herd crossed without breaking its lengthy line. The Red River was particularly dangerous to cross. It could rise rapidly, catching herds while they crossed.

had no choice but to wait until the water dropped. At one crossing, the Red River delayed sixty thousand cattle. When one of the herds stampeded a few nights later, all of the cattle for miles around ended up in a giant mill. It took ten days to separate the herds.[4]

Thieves

Sometimes, in southern Kansas, the trail herds were attacked by thieves. First the outlaws would try to frighten the trail crew into abandoning their livestock. Depending on the relative strengths of the trail crew and the thieves, the thieves might try to kill the trail crew outright. If neither goal could be accomplished, the gang would try to stampede the herd. This was easily done. At night, a gang member would sneak up to the herd. He would rise up and flap a buffalo robe or blanket, and the herd would rush off.

The members of the mob knew the lay of the land better than the cowboys did. The thieves moved all the cattle they could find to carefully chosen hiding places, where the cattle would remain hidden until it was safe for the gang to sell them as their own. If the pursuing trail crew caught up with them, the thieves would say that they had merely rounded up stampeded cattle that they planned to hold until the owners came for them.

Each night, cowboys spread out their bedrolls near the chuck wagon. They tethered (tied) their horses nearby.

Sometimes, more brazen thieves would return to the trail camp. They would announce how many heads they had, and ask for a set fee per head to return them.

South of the Red River, the Texas Rangers were a potent force in running down cattle thieves. In Kansas, a trail crew might be able to call on help from a posse or town officer. But in the Indian Territory, the cowboys were on their own. Even in Texas, not all officials were helpful. Some frontier officials posed as cattle inspectors and demanded a fee. Most herds expected to pay an inspection fee near the outset of their trip, but resented further meddling.

One trail boss dealt with the blackmail by offering the bogus inspector some beef in lieu of cash. He selected a monstrous steer and tied it to the tree with a frayed rope. The herd had barely left the area before

---

SOURCE DOCUMENT

MY FEET ARE IN THE STIRRUPS,
I AM SEATED IN MY SADDLE,
AS I RIDE AROUND
THESE DARNED OLD CATTLE.[5]

COME ALONG, BOYS, AND LISTEN TO MY TALE;
I'LL TELL YOU OF MY TROUBLES ON THE OLD CHISHOLM TRAIL.
COME A TI YI YIPPY, YIPPY YAY, YIPPY YAY,
COME A TI YI YIPPY, YIPPY YAY.[6]

To take their minds off of their hard work, cowboys would sometime sing these songs.

the steer rejoined the herd with a bit of broken rope around its horns.[7]

Getting the herd to Abilene was no guarantee of a profitable drive. In Kansas, the trail boss faced dangers of a different type. He had to decide to whom to sell his herd. He had three choices: He could sell to a speculator who would ship the herd to an eastern market. He could sell to a rancher from Colorado, Montana, Wyoming, or the Dakotas who would buy yearlings and two-year-olds for their herds. As the third option, the trail boss could hire a commission merchant to ship the beef directly to market. The first two choices involved the creditworthiness of the purchaser. Bad checks, forged bank drafts, and broken promises robbed many a herd owner of his reward. High freight rates and a sudden drop in cattle prices could destroy the profits of a drive for those who tried to market a herd themselves.

★ AMERICAN INDIANS ON THE CHISHOLM TRAIL ★

North of the Red River, the Chisholm Trail ran south to north through the Indian Territory (now Oklahoma). Here were the reservations of the Kiowa and Comanches, the Cheyenne and Arapaho. After 1870, just west of the trail near present-day Oklahoma City stood the storehouses, schoolhouse, and outbuildings of the Darlington Indian Agency. Travelers on the trail were impressed by the throngs of American Indians around the agency and the long strings of freight wagons that brought supplies to them.

The American Indians never succeeded in establishing a toll on the Chisholm Trail. In 1867, the Cherokees imposed a toll of ten cents a head on cattle crossing their lands on the Shawnee Trail. In 1871, the Creeks voted to tax herds 27½ cents a head. The tribes failed to collect the toll regularly. These levies helped dry up use of the Shawnee Trail in favor of the Chisholm Trail. The chance to escape the tolls was an argument used by Joseph McCoy when he urged Texas cattlemen to make the shift.

This did not mean that the herds passed through the Indian Territory without incident. Between the Red River and the Cimarron, a herd was likely to encounter a band of warriors. The warriors would assess the strength of the herd and cowboys and act accordingly. Sometimes they returned to the herd at night and caused a stampede. Then it was easy to drive off the horses and cattle they desired. Trail bosses soon learned that it was cheaper to give the warriors a few head of cattle than risk an attack. Most trail herds had picked up strays from other herds before reaching the Indian Territory. It was often these cattle that they gave up.

Sometimes a good bluff reduced the demand. One Kiowa chief demanded six steers. The trail boss offered two. The chief threatened, "Two not enough. You give me six or I'll come with my young braves tonight and stampede your cattle."

"Well," answered the boss, "when you come tonight, be sure to bring a spade. The cook broke the handle of our spade yesterday. When you come to stampede the cattle, I aim to kill you. Unless you bring a spade, we can't bury you." At that, the chief decided two steers were enough.[8]

The typical cattle drive up the Chisholm Trail lasted three to four months. By the time the cowboys reached the town at trail's end, their boots were worn out. Their hats were shapeless and caked with dust. The only people they had talked with were one another. They had seldom shaved, and they had bathed only in muddy streams. When

THE TOWNS AT THE END OF THE TRAIL

they were freed from their duties with the herd, the cowboys drew their pay. Their money would not burden them too long. The cowhands headed first for the barbershops and bathhouses. Then, clean and shaven, they would visit the haberdasher to buy new clothing. Only then, for a few glorious days, would they go on the town. They would try their luck at gambling and enjoy the offerings of the saloons. In general, they would go out looking to have a wild time.

In the towns, the townspeople and shop owners awaited the cowboys' coming, ready to separate trail hands from their money almost around the clock. They operated from false-front buildings. A false-front building is one in which the front extended beyond the dimensions of the actual building. This made the building seem larger than it actually was. These building were filled with marked-up goods. For the cowboys, the delights of the trail towns were truly wondrous. Steam locomotives hooted, and cattle cars clanked. A strolling street performer might fill the air with music. The saloon doors were open. From inside came the tinkle of pianos, the rattle of poker chips, and the voices of faro and monte dealers. The scrape of a fiddle announced a dance hall, where the cowhands could pair up for a few hours of foot-stomping dancing.

Well-dressed easterners filled the chairs on hotel porches, where the buyers and the Texans sealed their deals with a few words and a handshake. It did not take long for a cowboy to go broke. His money spent, he would remain in town. His pony might stand, reins hanging, outside a dry goods store. His trail boss was seated on a nearby bench, watching the activity. Sitting quietly, he might whittle with a jackknife for hours, until it was time to return to camp.

The townspeople were of two minds about the Texans. They knew they benefited from the cowboy's business. At the same time, a handful of "respectable" citizens projected an air of stern disapproval. Eventually, these residents would gain control of the town. They would pass ordinances that made the town unattractive to the cattle trade. Then the Texans would turn away, seeking another market. At various times, five different towns formed the end of the Chisholm Trail. Each, in turn, was to enjoy the title of "Cowboy Capital." Each boomed briefly, then lapsed into obscurity.

Abilene

For the Texas cowboy, Abilene, Kansas, offered a chance to ride in off the prairie into what one historian called "the delights of Hell." The town was thoroughly advertised, so sometimes a first-time visitor might be surprised at its small size. One Texas cowboy, standing in the middle of Texas Street, asked how far it was to Abilene. Told he was already there, he commented, "Well, I swan! I'd never seed such a little town have such a mighty big name."[1]

In 1867, Abilene was far from impressive. Before McCoy began building his hotel and livery stable, the

Texas cowboys found the energy to dance and celebrate after reaching Abilene.

biggest building in town was the Frontier Store. It measured eighteen feet by thirty feet. The shingled building served as post office, legal office, grocery store, and dry goods emporium. The two-story stage station lay west of town. Its second story sometimes served as the town dance hall. There was no train station. The outgoing mail sack hung from a post with a number on it. People who wanted to take the train stood nearby and signaled for the train. Obligingly, it stopped at the post.

In 1871, six hundred thousand cattle plodded north into Kansas. That year, Abilene boasted a year-round resident population of only eight hundred. Yet, the 1871 Census showed it possessed thirty-two places selling liquor. Five thousand parched Texas cowboys traveled up the Chisholm Trail that spring and summer. There were sixty-four gambling tables to accommodate them. Abilene's five general stores offered everything from diamonds to a pint of salt.

Yet for all its fame, Abilene would serve as the "Cowboy Capital" for only a few years. By 1872, Abilene was urging Texas herd owners to look elsewhere for a shipping point. Drovers, the people involved in cattle driving, would turn to Ellsworth farther west and Newton and Wichita farther south.

Ellsworth

Ellsworth was founded in 1867 near Fort Ellsworth/Harker. The settlement was named after Lieutenant Allen Ellsworth of the seventh Iowa Cavalry. People

---

SOURCE DOCUMENT

To Cattle Drovers:

We, the undersigned members of the Farmers' Protective Association and Officers and Citizens of Dickinson County, Kansas, most respectfully request all who have contemplated driving Texas Cattle to Abilene the coming season to seek some other point for shipment, as the inhabitants of Dickinson will no longer submit to the evils of the trade.[2]

This announcement mailed to Texas newspapers in 1872 told the ranchers to steer clear of Abilene. In its final printing, there were 366 signatures.

flocked there believing that the town would be the western terminus, or endpoint, of the Kansas Pacific Railroad. The merchants did business with the fifteen hundred soldiers and civilians at the fort, four miles from town.

The town got off to a shaky start. In June 1867, after a flash flood, Ellsworth found itself beneath four feet of water. In July, the townspeople suffered an outbreak of cholera. Three hundred died at the fort, fifty in town. Cheyenne raiders drove off large numbers of cattle from the town's outskirts. When the Kansas Pacific pushed farther west, many of the town's merchants went with it. The town's population shrank from almost one thousand to just forty.

Slowly the town built up again. In 1872, Ellsworth succeeded Abilene as the northern terminus of the Texas cattle trail. The herds reached the town by following a spur known as the Ellsworth Trail. This new trail branched from the old Chisholm Trail in Southern Kansas. For one year, Ellsworth was a rough-and-tough cow town. During that time, ten people were shot to death on the street or in gambling dens. That was all it took to convince the citizens of Ellsworth. The evils that accompanied the title of "Cowboy Capital" outweighed the benefits. When the herds went elsewhere the next year, the citizens of Ellsworth were much relieved.

Newton

Newton's history began in 1870 with the arrival of Judge R. W. P. Muse, a railroad agent representing the Atchison, Topeka & Santa Fe Railroad. The railroad was investigating possibilities for extending the line. Located on the Chisholm Trail, sixty-five miles south of Abilene, Newton seemed a very logical location for a Santa Fe Railroad terminal. By 1871, the new town had been born. It was named by a group of Santa Fe Railroad stockholders after their hometown of Newton, Massachusetts. With the completion of the railroad line in 1871, the railroad invited Joseph McCoy to Newton. They asked him to supervise the building of a stockyard.

Unlike some trail towns, cattle never roamed Newton's streets. McCoy built the pens a mile and a half to the west. Newton became the West's newest cow town. It soon became known as "Bloody and lawless—the wickedest city in the west."[3] It only enjoyed the cowboys' reign from June 1871 to January 1873. Completion of the Santa Fe Railroad to Dodge City and Wichita drew the cowboys to these places. In Newton, the railroad's completion ushered in times that were more peaceful.

Wichita

Wichita, seat of Sedgwick County, twenty-six miles south of Newton, was named for the Wichita people who originally inhabited the area. In 1864, J. R. Mead became the first white settler when he opened a trading post there. The following year, Jesse Chisholm

Among the Kansas Cattle towns, only Wichita, seen here in 1871, grew to become a large city. Today, Wichita's population is over three hundred thousand.

pioneered the Chisholm Trail. J. R. Mead had sent him into the Southwest with a wagonload of goods to trade with the Wichita for buffalo hides. Before the rails were laid to reach the town, Joseph McCoy and his associates built cattle pens there. In 1872, the town boasted a population of two thousand. A branch of the Santa Fe Railroad arrived at Wichita in that year. That was the signal for the town to "bust wide open." A sign at the outskirts of town proclaimed, EVERYTHING GOES IN WICHITA. The town's offerings included a raucous variety theater that featured women entertainers noted mostly for their lack of attire.

Wichita had better luck than the other cattle towns. It was able to deal with the worst elements of the cattle trade. Its lawmen managed to enforce the law. They reduced the number of killings during the years of its supremacy. Wichita boomed as a cow town until 1876, when settlers fenced off the prairie and the Chisholm Trail with barbed wire. Cattle drives shifted west to Dodge City. Unlike the other cattle capitals, Wichita grew large. Today it is a city with a population of over three hundred thousand.

Dodge City

Dodge City is located 150 miles west of Wichita. In 1871, H. L. Sitler constructed a sod house five miles west of Fort Dodge on the Santa Fe Trail. Within one year, this site grew into a town. It boasted a general store, three dance halls, and six saloons. The Santa Fe Railroad reached Dodge City in 1872. Texas cattle

Dodge City stores offered visiting cowboys a chance to relax and to buy new hardware and clothing.

drovers began to use a shortcut from the Chisholm Trail to Dodge City. They called it the Texas Trail. With these cattle came cowboys, gamblers, buffalo hunters, and soldiers. Dodge City became a rowdy town famous for its saloons, outlaws, and Boot Hill Cemetery.

The first city marshal was appointed in Dodge City after its incorporation in November 1875. The railroad tracks were known as the "dead line." Respectable saloons and businesses were located north of the tracks. To the south, lawmen made little effort to enforce ordinances unless a complaint was made or an actual fight broke out.

Often the mix of buffalo hunters, railroad workers, soldiers, and drifters settled their differences in shootouts. This created the need for a burial place. For six years, Dodge City did not have a cemetery. Those dying with friends, enough money, or sufficient standing in the community were buried in the post cemetery at Fort Dodge. Others, penniless or unknown, were buried wherever it was convenient to dig a hole. Boot Hill became the most famous burial ground in the West. It was used for only three years, 1875–78.

In 1876, Dodge City's population was twelve hundred. The number swelled during the summer with the influx of cowboys, buyers, gamblers, and prostitutes. Business houses, dance halls, and saloons catered to the Texas trade. Saloonkeepers renamed their places Nueces, Alamo, and Lone Star and served brandies, liqueurs, and the latest mixed drinks. Ice was usually available, so beer could be served cold. Some saloons advertised anchovies and Russian caviar on their lunch menus.

KANSAS COW TOWNS

TOWN	DATE	RAILROAD	CATTLE TRAIL
ABILENE	1867–72	KANSAS PACIFIC	CHISHOLM TRAIL
ELLSWORTH	1872–73	KANSAS PACIFIC	CHISHOLM/ELLSWORTH TRAILS
NEWTON	1871–72	SANTA FE	CHISHOLM TRAIL
WICHITA	1872–78	SANTA FE	CHISHOLM TRAIL
DODGE CITY	1875–85	SANTA FE	WESTERN/CHISHOLM TRAIL

A list of the five major cow towns, the cattle trail that led to them, and the railroad that was used to haul the beef east.

Gambling ranged from a game of five-cent Chuck-a-luck (a dice game) to thousand-dollar poker pots. Many saloons offered some type of musical entertainment. They ranged from a piano player or a singer to the five-piece orchestra in the Long Branch saloon.

By 1882, Dodge City was the last of Kansas's Cowboy Capitals. Its glory days were short. The final Texas cattle drives to Dodge City came in 1885. In the preceding decade, over 5 million cattle had been driven up the trail from Texas to Dodge City.

★ THE FRONTIER LAWMEN CONTROL THE ★ TEXAS COWBOYS

All the frontier towns in Kansas took a common action early in their history. The townspeople selected officers to uphold the law. There were three different categories of lawmen: The first type were federal marshals and their deputies who operated on a district-, state-, or territory-wide basis. They upheld federal laws and pursued escaped criminals and army deserters. Many federal officers served at the same time as city or county lawmen. Second, on the county level, the sheriff and his deputies enforced the law. From time to time, county lawmen swelled their ranks by swearing in local citizens as deputies and forming a posse. Last, at the city or town level, the city marshal served as the chief of police. Depending on the size of the town, the city marshal might be supported by a deputy marshal and a number of city policemen.

The Kansas cattle towns had two conflicting views on law enforcement as it applied to the visiting cowboys.

Cowboys could drink and gamble in the Long Branch saloon in Dodge City. In the saloon a five-piece orchestra offered musical entertainment.

They did not want to gain a reputation for strict law enforcement; that might discourage the trail herds from coming to their town. On the other hand, the local businesses existed to separate the cowboys from their wages as quickly as possible. That often included selling them a large quantity of liquor. The drunken revelers fired their pistols into the air, the ceiling, or each other. Many townspeople were content merely to keep out of range. If a lawman became involved with someone disturbing the peace, he was more likely to render the offender unconscious than to shoot him. After the offender sobered up in the local jail, a fine was duly collected. The cowboy returned home with a sore head, poorer and perhaps wiser.

Keeping law and order on the Kansas streets called for courage, skill, and a great deal of common sense. A major factor in the lawman's favor was the fame and reputation of the peace officer. Bat Masterson, Wyatt Earp, and Wild Bill Hickok all wore the lawman's star in Kansas. No matter how drunk, few cowboys were foolish enough to try to outdraw these stalwarts. Bat Masterson described the frontier lawmen he knew as ordinary men who could shoot straight. They also possessed, he added, courage and steady nerves, and a well-developed sense of right and wrong. They largely succeeded in keeping the cowboys from tearing their towns up by the roots before returning to Texas.

7

THE CLOSING OF THE CHISHOLM TRAIL

The end of the Chisholm Trail seemed likely as early as 1880. The route faced competition from other trails farther west. It was hemmed in by quarantine laws aimed at barring Texas cattle. Barbed wire fences threatened to bar the way permanently.

Caldwell Offers a Last Chance

In June 1880, the trail received a reprieve. The Santa Fe Railroad reached Caldwell, near the southern boundary of Kansas. The Chisholm Trail ran through Caldwell, close to the Indian Territory. Texas drovers could take cattle there without breaking the embargo they faced farther north. Texas herds soon arrived in Caldwell. The town quickly began taking business away from Dodge City. In its first year, Caldwell shipped 25,531 Texas steers to market. A year later, the figure climbed to 31,644. Caldwell doubled that figure in 1882. In this, its peak year, 64,007 Texas cattle were loaded on the Santa Fe trains in Caldwell.

Loaded on freight cars, cattle lost weight while on the way to eastern markets. The average shrinkage of cattle on a trip from Chicago to Boston was 10 to 15 percent.

In March 1883, the Cherokee Strip Live Stock Association served notice. Barbed wire fences closed the branches of the Chisholm Trail from Red Fork Ranch in the Indian Territory to Dodge City. The announcement pointed out that the Chisholm Trail was still open from the Red River to Caldwell. Nevertheless, many Texas cattle herds switched to the Western Trail. That route ran from Fort Griffin, Texas, to Dodge City.

There was a brief upsurge in 1884. The 57,112 cattle shipped from Caldwell included local cattle and animals raised in the Indian Territory. In the spring of 1885, the Santa Fe Railroad announced that it would no longer ship cattle from Caldwell. The owners of the railroad feared that the Texas cattle would infect the other cattle they carried.

The announcement virtually closed the Chisholm Trail. The closure took place less than twenty years after the first herds headed north to Abilene. A number of factors contributed to the end of this historic thoroughfare.

Changes In the Beef Industry

For almost twenty years, Texas cattle were shipped by rail from Kansas to Illinois. Those that were to be eaten in the Midwest were processed there. The rest were shipped live by train to eastern cities. The great distances involved were a major problem for the beef industry. The railroad equipment was primitive. Cars had no springs. They were equipped only with hand-operated brakes. The couplings between the cars caused jerks and jarring. The ballast (gravel) under the rails was uneven. Cattle were often jolted off their feet, bruised, and trampled. The cattle trains were poorly handled.

Animals often suffered from a lack of food and water. At rest stops along the long haul, steers were unloaded into pens. After eating and drinking, they were herded back aboard the cattle cars. This treatment caused cattle to lose weight quickly. The average shrinkage between Chicago and Boston was 10 to 15 percent.

One estimate placed the annual loss to cattlemen at $24 million.

Western beef was unpopular with the average customer in the east. It brought low prices. Though flavorful, longhorn beef was tough. After all, the animals had walked for months to reach the railhead. Some cattle buyers tried to obtain more tender meat. The cattle buyers fed the longhorns for several months on the lush grasses of the northern plains. Others tried to improve the longhorn stock by introducing European strains. Both efforts failed. On the Texas plains, the toughest and rangiest bulls outbred the weaker, fatter ones. This was true until barbed wire became common, when a rancher could breed his expensive bulls and keep the range stock out.

Using Refrigerator Cars

The first refrigerator cars appeared on the railroads in 1867. These double-walled iceboxes on wheels were not an immediate success. The meat became discolored after long contact with the ice. The beef also tended to spoil quickly after it was removed. Soon refrigerator cars appeared that kept the meat and ice in separate compartments. The cars had heavy insulated sides. This slowed the melting of the massive amounts of ice that cooled them. By 1869, refrigerator cars were carrying beef successfully from Chicago to Boston.

In 1875, cattle dealer Gustavus Swift moved to Chicago. From there, he began shipping processed

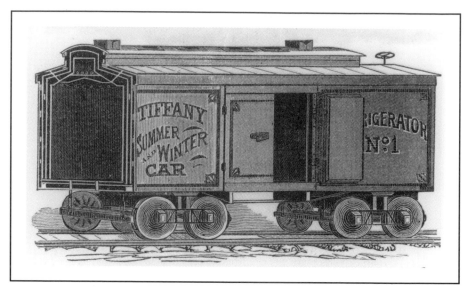

The development of refrigerator railroad cars ended the need to ship live cattle to market. The first refrigerator cars appeared in 1867. By 1869, refrigerator cars were successfully transporting beef from Chicago to Boston.

beef to eastern markets, using refrigerator cars. The railroad owners did not like the idea. Railroad owners made heavy revenues from hauling cattle, and they also had a big investment in cattle cars. They thought that refrigerator cars were hazardous and uncertain, and they refused to build the cars themselves. Swift had the resources to buy ten refrigerator cars on his own. Slowly, Swift & Company built up its fleet. The fleet peaked at five thousand refrigerator cars in 1926. The successful shipment of meat under refrigeration over long distances revolutionized the packing industry. Passing the longhorns by, the Chicago meatpackers began to seek heavier, fatter beef.

Two inventions allowed the production of other breeds of cattle in larger numbers:

Barbed Wire and Windmills

No one person invented barbed wire. Many inventors worked with the idea. In 1873, Illinois farmer Joseph F. Glidden was the first to apply for a specific patent. Glidden devised a simple machine to place barbs on wire. He made it from an old-fashioned coffee mill. For the first time, there was a practical way for farmers and ranchers to fence off their property. Glidden's double-strand design, "Winner," became the nation's best-selling barbed wire. Glidden protected his patent in lawsuits that reached all the way to the Supreme Court.

John W. Gates, a young hardware salesman, came to Texas in 1876. He was selling barbed wire for a Chicago firm, the Washburn-Moen Company. On his arrival in San Antonio, Gates set up a corral in a rented plaza. He invited ranchers to bring in their meanest fence-busters. Gates would prove that a slim strand of wire would hold them. He placed four sturdy posts upright in the ground. He connected three of them with a single strand of barbed wire. The longhorns were driven into the corral. Gates closed the fourth side with the wire. The longhorns attempted to break out. They repeatedly hurled themselves against the wire. The barbs bloodied their chests. The wire remained intact. Finally, the longhorns drew back defeated. The demonstration was a success. Gates returned to Illinois with more orders than the company could fill.

Barbed-wire fences were ideal for the treeless plains. Ranchers and farmers fenced off their holdings. Sales of barbed wire soared. Free grass and open trails began to disappear throughout the West. Some large cattle owners, accustomed to graze their cattle on the open range, objected to the fencing-off of small farms. For a few years, fence cutting and restringing bordered on open warfare. Finally, in 1884, Texas passed a rigid law making fence-cutting a felony.[1]

Although barbed wire allowed farms to be fenced, it was windmills that made them livable. In the 1880s, landowners were able to obtain low-priced iron windmills. They were both transportable and dependable. Advertisements proclaimed that windmills were the cheapest source of energy. Wells drilled into the semi-arid prairies tapped the water table below. Above the well sat the windmill. Its tower rose from twelve to twenty feet. Wooden vanes formed a wheel from six to ten feet in diameter. The prevailing winds turned the wheel of the windmill. A tail mechanism kept the wheel in position to catch the wind. Gears connected the wheel to a pump, located at ground level, which produced a constant flow of water. There was enough for the use of the family, their livestock, and a small garden.

The fenced off pastures and the dependable supply of water allowed farmers and ranchers to raise the breeds of cattle that would bring higher prices in the eastern markets.

The Quarantine Law of 1884

Kansas farmers had always been less than enthusiastic about the Texas longhorns that came up the Chisholm Trail. For years, the state of Kansas had passed quarantine laws. Gradually they expanded the portions of the state that were off-limits to Texas cattle. But in 1884, a final quarantine law helped close the Chisholm Trail for good. The new law prohibited all Texas cattle from entering the state between March 1 and December 1. This time frame included both the spring and fall trail-driving seasons. No Texas herds made it through to the Kansas railhead towns after that date. A few herds of cattle raised in Kansas were trailed to Dodge City for a year or two. A killing freeze during the winter of 1886–87 ended even that limited business.

The Railroads Spread Across Texas

At the same time, railroads were piercing deeper into Texas. After the Civil War, the state had only a few hundred miles of track. These lines were located along the Texas Gulf Coast. In 1872, the Missouri, Kansas, & Texas Railroad had entered Texas near Denton. The International and Great Northern Railroad was built south from the Red River toward the Rio Grande. The Texas and Pacific Railroad was built from east to west along the thirty-second parallel. The state encouraged railroad building. It gave the railroads large grants of public land. The railroads received construction loans from the state.

Packing plants met the demands of eastern customers for more tender beef.

Texas railroads offered the ranchers good shipping facilities. The railroads also offered favorable rates for livestock shipments. Potential buyers were attracted to the Texas railheads. Distances for cattle drives shrank. It was not necessary to cross the hundreds of miles separating Texas and Kansas. Now there was a Texas shipping point less than a hundred miles away.

A Last Effort

Some Texas cattlemen fought to preserve the future of the long drive. Between 1884 and 1886, they urged Congress to create a national trail that cattle could use to get to the northern railroads. Backers of the idea envisioned a route on federally owned land. No fences would block the way. The sponsors suggested a route that roughly followed the Western Trail. This route ran parallel with the Chisholm Trail, about one hundred twenty miles farther west. The creation of a national trail drew support from beef interests in Dodge City.

In September 1884, a national convention of livestock owners expanded on the idea. They asked Congress to layout and maintain a National Trail for cattle drives. The trail would run from the Red River to the Canadian border. This route would run through publicly owned lands. It would cross the Indian Territory, Kansas, Nebraska, and the Dakotas. The plan met with hostile reaction from Kansas. As a result, the delegates shifted the proposed route slightly. They moved it west to the eastern boundary of Colorado. Legislators from Texas introduced bills in both houses of Congress supporting the idea. It was also endorsed by the Texas legislature. Congress never voted on the idea. The bills died in committee.

By 1887, there were more cattle in Texas than there had been when the Chisholm Trail first opened. But there was no way to drive them north. Besides, the northern ranges were overstocked. Cattle prices were down. When southeastern Colorado was thrown open to settlement, homesteaders and their barbed-wire fences blocked the suggested route. The dream of an alternate route to the Chisholm Trail was dead.

★ TEXAS TICK FEVER: AN OLD PROBLEM ★ STILL UNSOLVED

Even before the Civil War, Texans had attempted to drive cattle to northern markets. In 1853, farmers and stockmen in western Missouri turned back a herd of three thousand Texas cattle heading for Westport (now Kansas City). They feared that the longhorns would infect their cattle with what the people from Missouri called "Texas fever." Years later, Kansas farmers shared these fears as Texas cattle streamed up the Chisholm Trail.

The disease did not originate in Texas. It was noted as early as 1796 in Pennsylvania and Virginia, carried there by cattle imported from South Carolina. These states banned importation of southern cattle between April and November (the ticks died in a cold winter climate). Texas fever outbreaks occurred in western Missouri as early as 1851. Local cattle, exposed to longhorns or placed on land the longhorns had occupied, became ill. Their backs arched. Their heads hung down. They staggered as they walked. Many died—the rest remained in poor health.

The cattlemen did not know the cause of Texas fever. The disease came from ticks carried by the Texas animals. The longhorns, though sometimes sickened by the disease, did not die of it, as did the Missouri cattle. The ticks were transmitted to the cattle through deer. Tick fever usually affects cattle and other hoofed animals. It affects only some humans—only those who have had their spleen removed.

Texas tick fever was declared eradicated in the United States in 1943. Quarantining the cattle, vacating pastures, and dipping cattle into large vats of pesticide-treated water accomplished the job. But today, with trade between the United States and Mexico increasing, the old problem of Texas fever has become new again. In Mexico, the disease is still prevalent. Presently, there is a two-mile-wide strip of quarantined land along the Texas border from Del Rio, Texas, to the mouth of the Rio Grande. This land serves as a buffer zone to prevent the reestablishment of the ticks in Texas. That is only part of the problem. When American cattle are imported into Mexico, 40 to 50 percent of them may die within a few months from tick fever. Scientists at Texas A & M University are working to develop a vaccine that will give inoculated animals immunity to the disease.

8

THE LEGACY OF THE CHISHOLM TRAIL

Herds moved up the Chisholm Trail from 1867 to 1884. More than a century has passed since, but the way of life and events of those few years has remained a part of America's consciousness.

The Longhorns

In 1890, there were 60 million cattle in the United States. Most contained Texas longhorn blood. At that time, ranchers began to breed cattle selectively. After 1900, purebred cattle from Europe and Asia became available. These breeds produced heavier animals with more tender meat. Most ranchers chose to breed up. The number of longhorns plunged.

Before 1900, candles made from tallow were the chief source of light. Tallow is obtained by melting down animal fat. The making of soaps, lubricants, and cooking oil also required tallow. Cattle buyers preferred heavy tallow-producing animals. Longhorns are naturally lean. They have 80 percent less tallow than English breeds. The demand for longhorns diminished further. The Texas longhorn came close to extinction.

The Windmill allowed settlers to set up new farms along the route of the Chisholm Trail. Windmills, which were quite affordable by the late 1880s, provided energy.

In 1927, the United States government realized the longhorn's end was near. It established a longhorn herd at the Wichita Mountains Wildlife Refuge, in Cache, Oklahoma. The herd became the basis for the breed's preservation. Today, longhorn breeders have a choice. They can raise animals with a pure bloodline. If they wish, they can mix several family bloodlines.

Over the years, food trends change. People today seek healthier foods. High-protein lean meat is a premium item. Breeders are quick to respond to demand, and longhorns are again in favor. The trend is not limited to this country. Foreign investors are purchasing longhorn breeding stock. Many breeders and hobbyists are again breeding longhorns. Today, a longhorn heifer costs about a thousand dollars. A bull can bring several times that.

The Mustangs

Vast herds of mustangs once ranged across the American West. They do so no longer. Working cowboys depended on capturing, breaking, and riding mustangs. Today, cowboys have replaced them with cutting horses, ropers, and quarter horses of many different breeds.

Mustangs roam wild in only a few limited areas of the West. Most live on government-managed lands. The mustangs overgrazed these limited grasslands. The government studied the problem. The solution was to reduce their number. The government did not want to slaughter them, so it began to round up the mustangs. Using aircraft and riders, it drove the mustangs into corrals. The government then made the mustangs available to the public.

Congress began the adoption program in 1971. It later created a system of legal titles: An adopter would keep each animal for one year. Then, after complying with a health check, the adopter got title. Until the title was issued, the animal remained government property. Under the program, the Bureau of Land Management (BLM) has captured 165,000 mustangs and burros. It has handed over most of them to adopters for $125 each. Only about forty thousand mustangs still roam the western United States.

The Cowboy

American cowboys did not vanish with the trail herds. They are alive and well as never before. Consider these figures for just one state: There are five thousand members in the Oklahoma Cattlemen's Association. Each has cowboys and cowgirls who work for them. In the 1990s, Oklahoma had 5.6 million cattle. The state counted seventy thousand horses (not counting

Herds coming up the Chisholm Trail were sometimes blocked by barbed-wire fences. Longhorns who tried to break through the barbed wire were severely cut by the barbs.

racehorses). The state had over 15 million acres of pasture. Beef cattle accounted for about $2 billion annually in sales.

A Continuing Romance

The love affair with the American cowboy began with the dime novels of the late 1800s. This enthusiasm spread with the help of the dozens of novels written by Zane Grey. America's fascination with cowboys blossomed anew as audiences crowded into silent movies that depicted the West.

Today, there are countless cowboy-related businesses. Western wear is available nationwide and Western music floods the airwaves. Western art fills galleries and museums. Films depicting the Old West abound in theaters and on television. Western fans subscribe to national publications such as *True West* magazine. Western themes fill thousands of works of fiction and nonfiction. These writings are churned out by successful hacks as well as scholars. There are thirty dude ranches in Oklahoma alone. People come and pretend they are cowboys. Add to this the festivals and symposia, poetry sessions and such goings on around the country, all with cowboys as the theme.

The movies have zeroed in on the Chisholm Trail. A black-and-white "B" movie, *The Old Chisholm Trail*, was filmed in 1943 by Universal Pictures. Directed by Elmer Clifton, it included the four standard roles found in the genre. The action hero was played by Johnny Mack Brown. Tex Ritter played the singing cowboy.

Dipping Cattle

A.A.Forbes Photo

Ranchers dipped their cattle into large vats of pesticide-treated water to destroy ticks. Despite this, Kansas outlawed the Texas trail herds.

Fuzzy Knight acted the role of the hero's sidekick. Jennifer Holt provided the romantic interest. *Red River* (1948) is a classic Western. It is considered by many critics to be one of the ten best films ever made. The movie was directed by Howard Hawks and starred John Wayne and Montgomery Clift. It is a sweeping, epic story about a cattle drive at the time of the opening of the old Chisholm Trail.

America's embrace of the cowboy extends from coast to coast. Millions are learning western line dancing. People dance the Texas two-step, Cotton Eye Joe, and the Achy-Breaky Heart. Cable television channels broadcast cowboy songs seven days a week. Regardless of their origin, country music performers don cowboy boots, jeans, fringed vests, and Stetsons. They travel in private buses to fairs, dance halls, rodeos, and clubs nationwide. Throughout the country, audiences pack rodeo grounds. They watch cowboys compete in roping, bulldogging, and bronco and bull riding events.

Preserving the Chisholm Trail Heritage

The Chisholm Trail crossed Texas, Oklahoma, and Kansas. Each has many reminders today of the herds that once passed through them. Three trail towns in Kansas have preserved at least a portion of their towns as they were in the trail driving days. Old Dodge City is a Western history museum located on the original site of the Boot Hill Cemetery. The recreation of Dodge City's main street as it looked in the 1870s features stagecoach rides and gunfight reenactments. There is also a recreation of the Boot Hill cemetery nearby.

Wichita has a seventeen-acre open-air history museum, Old Cowtown Museum. It is open from March to October. It features daily life in a Kansas cattle town on the Chisholm Trail.

Old Abilene Town & Museum recreates the Texas Street of the Abilene cow town. On weekends, from Memorial Day to Labor Day, it features reenactments of gunfights and stagecoach rides. It also contains a museum, reconstructed stores, and a church, school, and train station.

Museums abound on the Chisholm Trail route. In Wellington, Kansas, the Chisholm Trail Museum has forty rooms of artifacts and pictures. In Oklahoma, the Chisholm Trail Historical Museum at Waurika, competes with the Chisholm Trail Historical Museum in Kingfisher. Near the Chisholm Trail Museum in Duncan, Oklahoma, is *On the Chisholm Trail*, a monument to the American Cowboy, a fairly accurate representation of the beginning of a day's journey on the Chisholm Trail.

The Oklahoma State Legislature, in 1996, designated U.S. Route 81 as the Chisholm Trail Historic Route. The highway roughly parallels the old trail, all the way from the Red River into Kansas. Markers have been set in place from the Red River to the Kansas border. They show where the Chisholm Trail once passed. Motorists on U.S. 81 south of Caldwell, Kansas, are reminded of the Chisholm Trail in a different way. On the bluff to the east, they see the Ghost Riders of the Chisholm Trail. The silhouette is astride the actual Chisholm Trail. It was completed in 1995 after hundreds of hours of volunteered labor, land, and donations. The scene is lifelike. Observers are certain they have noticed both dust and sounds coming from the bluff area.

Many of the towns and cities along the trail remember the Chisholm Trail each year with special events. For over twenty years, Fort Worth, Texas, has celebrated a three-day event, the Chisholm Trail Round Up. Among others are the Chisholm Trail Festival in Yukon, Oklahoma, the Chisholm Trail Celebrations in Clearwater, Kansas, and Caldwell, Kansas.

Two quotations on display at the Chisholm Trail Exhibit in Wichita's Sedgwick County Historical Museum sum up the impact of this historic trail. One says, "Much of the legend of the American cowboy was born on the Chisholm Trail." The other reads, "The Chisholm Trail did not just lead from Mexico to Kansas, it led from yesterday to tomorrow."[1]

★ ROUND ROCK HONORS THE CHISHOLM TRAIL ★

Round Rock is a town twenty miles north of Austin in central Texas. Established in 1850, the town was named for a large round rock in bed of Brushy Creek. The Chisholm Trail later crossed the stream beside that landmark. The low water crossing had gradual banks and a limestone bottom. The village boasted several buildings built of the local stone. They included a stage depot (now a restaurant), a general store, and a handful of inns. The St. Charles Hotel, built in 1850, still operates as a bed-and-breakfast inn today.

When the drives began in South Texas, the range-bred longhorns were spooky—meaning they were quick to stampede, and hard to handle. It took every rider the ranches could muster to control the herd. By the time the herds reached Round Rock, the cattle had learned what was expected of them on the trail. Some riders could return to manage the ranch. The others, called Kansas men, would make the trip to Abilene. In 1867, thirty-five thousand men moved up the trail as they passed through Round Rock's Williamson County.

In the central Texas area, the Chisholm Trail served as a marker of another kind. East of the trail stretched the black soil of the South. It was watered by thirty-five inches of annual rainfall, adequate for growing cotton without irrigation. West of the trail lay the limestone outcroppings of the Edwards Plateau and the Hill Country, where thin topsoil allows only grazing and an occasional orchard. This line of demarcation marked the start of the American West.

During the days of the Chisholm Trail, an event occurred that brought Round Rock to national attention. The town was the site of the killing of the notorious outlaw Sam Bass, now buried in Round Rock Cemetery. Bass's gang's robberies plagued stagecoaches, trains, and banks in the area and was the object of an intensive chase by the Texas Rangers. An informer warned the Rangers and Round Rock lawmen of a planned raid on a local bank. The Bass gang was ambushed there on July 18, 1878. Wounded in the gun battle, Sam Bass died two days later.

Recently, the City of Round Rock and the Round Rock Chamber of Commerce commissioned artist Jim Thomas to cast a series of eighteen life-size bronze sculptures. The sculptures represent a cattle drive up the Chisholm Trail. They will include longhorn steers, calves, cowboys on horseback, and a campsite. The figures will be placed at the round rock in 2002.

★ TIMELINE ★

1521—First shipment of cattle from Spain to Mexico.

1805 **or 1806**—Jesse Chisholm is born in Tennessee.

1836—Texas wins independence from Mexico.

1861—Kansas becomes a state.

1861 **–1865**—Civil War.

1862—Homestead Act offers any citizen one hundred sixty acres of surveyed public land.

1865—Chicago stockyards open.

1866—Transatlantic cable is laid down, linking Europe to North America.

1867—The first refrigerator cars appear on the railroads.

1867 **–1872**—Abilene, Kansas, is the most northern destination on the Chisholm Trail for cattle from Texas.

1868—Jesse Chisholm dies.

1871 **–1872**—Newton is a terminus on the Chisholm Trail.

1872—Santa Fe Railroad reaches Dodge City.

1872 **–1873**—Ellsworth is established as a terminus on the Ellsworth cattle trail.

1872 **–1878**—Wichita is the terminus on the Chisholm Trail.

1875—Fort Reno is built.

1875—Dodge City is the terminus on the Texas cattle
–1885   trail.

1880—Caldwell is the terminus on the Chisholm
–1884   Trail.

1884—Kansas quarantine law leads to closing of the
        Chisholm Trail.

1927—Government establishes a longhorn herd at the
        Wichita Mountains Wildlife Refuge in Cache,
        Oklahoma.

1943—The movie, *The Old Chisholm Trail*, is released.

1996—Oklahoma State Legislature designates U.S.
        Route 81 as the Chisholm Trail Historic
        Route.

★ CHAPTER NOTES ★

Chapter 1. Joseph McCoy Has a Vision

1. Wayne Gard, *The Chisholm Trail* (Norman, Okla: University of Oklahoma Press, 1954), p. 63.

2. Henry Jameson, *Miracle of the Chisholm Trail* (Abilene, Kans.: Tri-State Chisholm Trail Centennial Commission, 1967), pp. 16–17.

3. Dee Brown, *Trail Driving Days* (New York: Charles Scribner's Sons, 1974), p. 9.

4. David Dary, *Cowboy Culture* (New York: Alfred A. Knopf, 1981), p. 184.

5. Ibid., p. 231.

6. Joseph G. McCoy, "Cattle Trade of the West and Southwest," Chapter 3 of *Kansas Collection Books*, 1874, <http://kuhttp.cc.ukans.edu/carrie/kancoll/books/mccoy/mcchap03.htm> (May 11, 1999).

7. Sam Ridings, *The Chisholm Trail* (Guthrie, Okla.: Co-Operative Publishing Co., 1936), p. 22.

Chapter 2. The United States in 1867

1. Henry S. Commager, *Documents of American History* (New York: F. S. Crofts & Co., 1945), vol. 2, pp. 38–39.

2. *Historical Statistics of the United States* (Washington, D.C.: U.S. Department of Commerce, 1960), p. 14.

3. Wesley S. Griswold, *A Work of Giants: Building the First Transcontinental Railroad* (New York: McGraw Hill, 1962), p. 230.

4. *Historical Statistics*, p. 737.

5. Henry S. Commager, *Documents of American History* (New York: F. S. Crofts & Co., 1945), vol. 1, pp. 410–411.

Chapter 3. Cattle Roundup in South Texas

1. Dee Brown, *Trail Driving Days* (New York: Ballantine Books, 1974), pp. 1–2.

2. Charles A. Siringo, *A Texas Cowboy* (Lincoln: University of Nebraska Press, 1950), pp. 48–49.

3. *Ladino* is a cowboy slang term for an outlaw animal, one that refuses to join the herd.

4. Frank J. Dobie, *The Longhorns* (New York: Bramhall House, 1941), pp. 319–320.

5. Tom Lea, *The King Ranch* (Boston: Little Brown and Co., 1957), vol. 1, pp. 320–321.

Chapter 4. Life on the Trail

1. Time-Life Books, *The Cowboys* (Alexandria, Va.: Time-Life Books, 1974), p. 18.

2. Wayne Gard, *The Chisholm Trail* (Norman: University of Oklahoma Press, 1954), p. 109.

3. Charles A. Siringo, *A Texas Cowboy* (Lincoln: University of Nebraska Press, 1950), p. 59.

Chapter 5. Hazards of the Trail

1. Wayne Gard, *The Chisholm Trail* (Norman: University of Oklahoma Press, 1954), p. 126.

2. Ibid.

3. Sam P. Ridings, *The Chisholm Trail* (Guthrie, Okla.: Co-operative Publishing Co., 1936), p. 366.

4. Don Worcester, *The Chisholm Trail* (Lincoln: University of Nebraska Press, 1980), pp. 57–59.

5. Ridings, p. 356.

6. Gard, p. 248.

7. Ibid., p. 128.

8. Ibid., pp. 130–131.

Chapter 6. The Towns at the End of the Trail

1. Henry B. Jameson, *Miracle of the Chisholm Trail* (Abilene, Kans.: Tri-State Chisholm Trail Centennial Commission, 1973), p. 26.

2. Robert Dykstra, *The Cattle Towns* (New York: Atheneum, 1970), p. 304.

3. David Dary, *Cowboy Culture* (New York: Alfred A. Knopf, 1981), p. 207.

Chapter 7. The Closing of the Chisholm Trail

1. David Dary, *Cowboy Culture* (New York, Alfred A. Knopf, 1981), p. 321.

Chapter 8. The Legacy of the Chisholm Trail

1. "Chisholm Trail Exhibit," *Wichita Sedgwick Co. Historical Museum*, n.d., <http://www.wichita-cvb.org/wht/site7.html> (May 11, 1999).

★ FURTHER READING ★

Brown, Dee. *Trail Driving Days*. New York: Charles Scribner's Sons, 1974.

Cushman, Ralph. *Jesse Chisholm*. Austin, Tex.: Eakin Press, 1992.

Dary, David. *Cowboy Culture*. New York: Alfred A. Knopf, 1981.

Dykstra, Robert J. *The Cattle Towns*. New York: Athenaeum, 1970.

Flanagan, Sue. *Trailing the Longhorns, a Century Later*. Austin, Tex.: Madrona Press, 1974.

Gard, Wayne. *The Chisholm Trail*. Norman: University of Oklahoma Press, 1954.

Jameson, Henry. *Miracle of the Chisholm Trail*. Abilene, Kans.: Tri-State Chisholm Trail Centennial Commission, 1967.

Mora, Jo. *Trail Dust and Saddle Leather*. New York: Charles Scribner's Sons, 1950.

Ridings, Sam. *The Chisholm Trail*. Guthrie, Okla.: Co-Operative Publishing Co., 1936.

Siringo, Charles A. *A Texas Cowboy*. Lincoln: University of Nebraska, 1950.

Time-Life Books. *The Cowboys*. Alexandria, Va.: Time-Life Books, 1973.

———. *The Gunslingers*. Alexandria, Va.: Time-Life Books, 1974.

———. *The Townsmen*. Alexandria, Va.: Time-Life Books, 1975.

Worcester, Don. *The Chisholm Trail*. Lincoln: University of Nebraska Press, 1980.

Internet Addresses

Kelly, Jim. *The Trail to Abilene*. 1996. <http://ktwu.wuacc.edu/journeys/articles/chisholm.html> (January 3, 2000).

Maloney, Ann, ed. *The Chisholm Trail and Overland Cattle Trade*. n.d. <http://users.rootsweb.com/~oknowata/TCT.htm> (January 3, 2000).

Rossel, John. *Chisholm Trail Timeline*. 1936. <http://www.kshs.org/perspect/chisholm.htm> (January 3, 2000).

The Shawnee News-Star. *Chisholm Trail Celebrates 130th Anniversary*. 1997. <http://www.news-star.com/stories/092097/arts_chisholm.html> (January 3, 2000).

Wichita Sedwick Co. Historical Museum. *Chisholm Trail Exhibit*. n.d. <http://www.wichita-cvb.org/wht/site7.html> (January 3, 2000).

★ INDEX ★